The Weekend Marketer

Say Goodbye to the '9 to 5',
Build an Online Business,
and
Live the Lifestyle You Love

Other Books by Connie Ragen Green:

Huge Profits With a Tiny List: 50 Ways to Use Relationship Marketing to Increase Your Bottom Line

Huge Profits With Affiliate Marketing: How to Build an Online Empire by Recommending What You Love

Article Marketing: How to Attract New Prospects, Create Products, and Increase Your Income

Membership Sites Made Simple: Start Your Own Membership Site for Passive Online Income

Targeted Traffic Techniques for Affiliate Marketers

By Connie Ragen Green and Geoff Hoff:

The Inner Game of Internet Marketing

Time Management Strategies for Entrepreneurs: How to Manage Your Time to Increase Your Bottom Line

The Weekend Marketer

**Say Goodbye to the '9 to 5',
Build an Online Business,
and
Live the Lifestyle You Love**

**By
Connie Ragen Green**

Copyright © 2012 by Hunter's Moon Publishing
ISBN: 978-1-937988-05-0

Hunter's Moon Publishing

Photography by Tony Laidig
Cover design by Shawn Hansen

Dedication

Dedicated to anyone who has ever looked out the window while at work and wished they did not have to be there; to people everywhere who are working at jobs that do not allow them to express their own creative ideas or reach their full potential; and to those who no longer have a job and still need to earn a full-time income to provide for themselves and their families. You are a Weekend Marketer™ at heart, and this book will provide the tools for you to change your life forever.

Table of Contents

Foreword

A little over seven years ago, in April of 2005, something happened that, unbeknownst to me at that time, would brighten my life for years to come and brighten the lives of so many others beyond what I could have ever imagined.

On that day, I gave a presentation at the Learning Annex Real Estate Expo in Los Angeles. There were over 10,000 eager participants in the huge conference center, but this story is not about them. It was roughly my 5,000th speech in my 27 years on stage as a professional speaker, but this story is not about me. This story is about one shy young broke, but hopeful, lady who was listening more intently than possibly anyone else in the hall. Little did I know that I would make such an impact on that one particular woman in the audience that day, and that I would go on to have such a deep relationship with her.

I don't remember Connie from that day, but she was there, somewhere in the audience. She purchased my Monthly Mentor® program and took the large box of materials home. She also registered for my Wealth Creator Source™ series of monthly interviews. I learned later that every month during the next year she faithfully followed my instructions, reorganized her life, cleaned her messes, and set and achieved her goals, one by one.

This wonderful woman was Connie Ragen Green.

I did not actually get to meet her until a year later. I was again speaking at an event in Los Angeles, and she rose to give me a testimonial. She told the audience that she had been able to completely change her life through my mentoring. I was so happy to hear of her wonderful achievements. She had left her job as a classroom teacher, moved to a city twenty miles from where she had been living for thirteen years, and started her own business. Every area of her life had dramatically improved.

Many of my students experience profound results, but usually I do hear their results in person. Hearing Connie's story made me realize what I already knew: The Monthly Mentor® changes lives in profound ways.

Years later, I was giving a speech in Atlanta. To my amazement and joy, I learned that one of my fellow speakers was going to be Connie! I felt like a proud Dad. I listened to and greatly enjoyed her speech, but felt that she was not delivering her genius well to the participants. She had so much to offer, but they weren't getting it. As she had only just begun to speak at live events, I decided to again take her under my wing and help her with her presentation. I realized that her gift was helping little people do really well on the Internet but her presentation was not getting across that message. So I named her program for her – <u>How To Make Huge Money With A Tiny List</u> – and she loved it. That was the beginning of her successful teaching career.

Within a month she started a blog: **http://HugeProfitsTinyList.com** and totally revised her presentation.

So, the first time we were together, I helped her launch her Internet business and change her life. The second time, I helped her launch her Internet *teaching* business and change her life again. But wait, there's more.

In the summer of 2009, in Las Vegas, I was a speaker at Armand Morin's Big Seminar. Not only was Connie there and not only was she a speaker, she was in competition for the "Better Your Best" Contest. She was one of the stars!

I was spell-bound as she told her story of transforming herself from an over-worked unhappy broke going-nowhere life to living a self-designed joyous life of luxury and service to others. The audience was enrapt. Her message broke through right into their hearts. How do I know? Firstly, I myself was crying. Secondly, when the votes were counted, she was named the winner of the contest. She took home the grand prize that night – twenty-five thousand dollars in cash – plus the honor of representing Armand Morin, one of the foremost Internet marketers in the world, as his Ambassador during the coming year.

Most recently, Connie joined me on my stage in Toronto to speak at my very first Ultimate Author Boot Camp. She mesmerized the audience of several hundred people with her story of how she has come so far over these past seven years, and how becoming a published author, not once, but many times has changed her life forever.

Her story resonated with every single person there, and they gave her a standing ovation for the information she shared with them that weekend. Her gracious and generous ways are a tribute to authors everywhere, and she will now be speaking at many of my upcoming events around the world over the next two years.

When she told me she was writing yet another book, I was overjoyed, particularly when she gave me the deep honor of writing this Foreword. Again I feel like a proud Dad watching Connie grow, spread her wings, and help others. To have been some part in each of the huge profound changes in Connie's life and to see how she is enlivening those around her is one of the greatest joys of my life. Connie is a special soul whose candle fortunately shines so brightly now and lights so many other candles.

She may well feel blessed by me; but more importantly, her clients and readers of this book are blessed by being able to receive her wisdom and love.

Raymond Aaron
New York Times Bestselling Author
Founder, Ultimate Author Boot Camp
http://UltimateAuthorsBootCamp.com

Introduction

Today you are you,
that is truer than true.
There is no one alive
who is youer than you.
~Dr. Seuss

We are all just ordinary people doing extraordinary things in our daily lives. This has been my belief for some time now, and I'll explain exactly what I mean by this statement. Since starting my online business at the end of 2005 I have met people from around the world who are changing their lives and the lives of others around them and throughout the world one day at a time. They are the true heroes of this era in our world's history and deserve the utmost respect for their courage and the actions they take on a day to day basis. I've met some of these people online, others at live events related to online marketing, and others through the charities and non-profit organizations I have been a part of for the past seven years.

My wish for you is that you would go through this book in a methodical and determined way. Instead of just reading straight through from beginning to end, take your time and make lots of notes for yourself as you explore the realm of possibilities presented here. Ask yourself along the way 'What is the next logical step for me?'

The ideas for books have many origins, and this one is no different. This is my fourteenth book, including five I have written on my own, two I penned with a co-author, and six where I contributed a chapter or a section along with several other authors.

Like many people, I had always wanted to write a book. I had no idea what my book would be about, but over the years I made some notes and brainstormed some ideas. When I made the decision to come online in 2005, leading to actions that would ultimately change my life forever, I thought of what I was doing as *running my life like a business*. I registered that domain name and started writing the story of how I was changing my life, from one of lack and mediocrity, to one of abundance and excellence in order to live a life I did not even know existed.

I actually began writing my first book during the spring of 2006. I sat down at my computer and just began writing. Little did I know at the time that this was not the way to go about writing a book, or writing anything, for that matter. Without an outline or any idea of what I truly wanted to achieve with this writing my book was doomed from the start. I went back to writing articles and blog posts and gave up on the idea of writing a book at that time. This was only a temporary setback, as I was determined to become a published author and sought out people and programs to help me turn my ideas into a worthwhile book.

By 2010 I had completed that first book – *Huge Profits With A Tiny List: 50 Ways To Use Relationship Marketing To Increase Your Bottom Line*. This book was so well received that I was encouraged to write my second book on affiliate marketing just a year later, and within two more years I had written several more books and contributed to countless others.

The book you are reading now is the culmination of my experiences since the very beginning of making the decision to get started on the Internet as an online entrepreneur. I had worked as a classroom teacher for twenty years, and, simultaneously worked in real estate as a residential appraiser and listing broker. I longed for a way to work from home, and after a serious work injury and bouts with cancer I was more determined than ever to make this a reality.

My prayer each day was to be able to work from my bedroom if necessary, and to be able to earn enough money to meet all of my financial obligations with grace and ease. God answered my prayer and now I am fortunate enough to be able to share what I do with people around the world who need this blessing in their life as well.

As you make your way through the book, remember that your journey will be a unique one. If you decide to take action and implement what I am sharing here you will become one more ordinary person living an extraordinary life.

Section One

What is a 'Weekend Marketer'?

Each of us must experience one of two pains - the pain of discipline or the pain of regret. Which pain will you choose? ~Jim Rohn

This concept of working on the weekend to improve your life is not a new one. In fact, people have utilized the opportunity of working at two different jobs at least since the time of the Industrial Revolution. This was the period in our world's history from 1750 to 1850 where changes in manufacturing, agriculture, transportation, and technology had a powerful effect on the economic and social conditions that were prevalent at the time. The invention of the rotary printing press, starting in 1843, solidified the cultural change that was about to take place.

Those who had worked on farms came looking for work in the cities, and many of these workers returned to the farm on the weekends in order to ensure a better life for themselves as well as for those who remained on the farm.

You may have also heard the terms 'moonlighting' and 'sidelining' in reference to those who work at a second job to earn additional income, to learn new skills, or to pursue a path that has always appealed to them.

In the 21st Century it is not uncommon for someone to go back to school or start a business after working at one or more previous jobs or careers for a number of years. Being able to embark on such a journey is life-changing in many cases.

Why You Must Have A Way To Earn Money Other Than From Your Job

This last recession was hard on everyone. Whether you lost your job during this time, believed you might lose your job, or still have your job, what I am going to say may make you do a double take.

Most jobs, in the purest sense of what that word implies in North America, are not healthy, natural, or fun. Some jobs may even be dangerous to your health and well-being. Allow me to explain what I mean by this.

For more than twenty years I worked as a classroom teacher in the greater Los Angeles area. This meant that I got up each morning around four-thirty and left my house by a quarter until six to avoid the rush hour traffic as much as possible. I would arrive at school by six-thirty and come in through the side gate right behind the custodian. Then I would spend the next half hour setting up my room, greeting the students and teachers as they arrived, and preparing for my day.

The school had been built during the 1950s, and then bungalows added during the 70s and 80s. This meant that we had asbestos in the flooring and ceiling tiles, and many teachers wore masks to avoid the harmful fumes. I never seemed to have any problem with this, but eventually I had huge medical problems. There will never be any way of knowing if my health issues were related to any of this.

After school each day, which was around three or three-thirty most days, I would drive to my real estate appointments. I worked as a residential appraiser and a listing broker, so I was involved in a variety of activities related to these positions. During the summer months I worked until at least eight o'clock because I had enough light to see what I was doing. Day in, day out turned into year in, year out for me, and my life was passing me by.

This was an extremely stressful lifestyle, but over the years I came to believe that this was the only way for me to be a productive member of society and meet all of my financial obligations. I had returned to college at age thirty in order to pursue my teaching credential, so no one had coerced me into this career and its demands. Yet, down deep inside I knew that something would have to change if I were to feel that I was leading the life God had intended for me.

After being diagnosed with cancer for the first time in 1992 at the age of thirty-seven I began to think about changing my life, but at that time I just couldn't see a way to be able to do it. The only people I was spending any time with were either teachers or those working in some aspect of real estate. I see now having no friends outside of my circle was keeping me from expanding my thinking.

My belief during that period of my life was that you had to work hard until you reached retirement age. This was still a harsh reality in my way of thinking, so I just stepped back from these thoughts about changing my life and went back to work as soon as possible. We can only do what we know and become aware of, and working as an online entrepreneur was not something I had ever heard about, as far as I knew.

There isn't a job anywhere that will pay me what I am able to earn online, while making my own hours and working from any location in the world. Add this to the fact that I have made myself unemployable over these past few years by taking myself out of the work force and becoming an entrepreneur, and earning an excellent living from my online endeavors is even more attractive. I believe anyone can do this, even though it may not be appealing for you right now if you are at a job you truly enjoy.

If you have a job that you absolutely love, and many people do, or if you are five years or less from retirement from your job, then you fall into a special category. You should continue reading to learn how to enhance your retirement and to have more control over your life between now and then, but don't just quit or resign from your job until you have a solid plan. That would not be a good idea, so it would not be prudent of me to even suggest it here.

You can greatly simplify your life by becoming an online entrepreneur. Being able to work from home allows you to avoid the early morning rush to get ready to leave for work, the traffic to and from your job, interactions with people throughout the day, and much more. You will be able to spend more time with family and friends, get involved with your local community and other organizations, and spend your time on your own schedule instead of someone else's time frame. I used to commute three to four hours each day, so just saving that time each week once I was working from home made a huge difference in my life.

Why Everyone Should Become An Entrepreneur

Becoming an online entrepreneur is an opportunity that has only been around since the mid to late 1990s. Back then there were only a few brave souls who were willing to test the waters and find out just what this could mean to people who wanted to start a business using the new technologies that were just coming of age.

During this time I was working as a classroom teacher and also in real estate, so even though I was using computers on a daily basis I never thought of this as a way to earn a living. It was people like Marlon Sanders and Dr. Jeanette Cates, both of whom I now count as good friends, who paved the way for doing business on what would become the Internet within a few years. I always tease them about being the ones who invented the Internet, along with Al Gore.

The turn of the century marked the point in time where many people began exploring this exciting and promising new world. This is right around the time when I began looking at the sites set up by the major retailers to find out what they had available for sale in their stores. I was not aware of anyone making purchases directly through these websites, but it must have become available in some form around this time.

Companies such as Sears, JC Penney, and Montgomery Ward were on the forefront of this revolutionary new marketing strategy, and other retailers soon followed in their footsteps with innovative ways to help customers consume more of their goods. Companies such as United Parcel Service and Federal Express were also gearing up to meet the growing demand for easy shipping as people began to order goods and have them delivered to their door.

I was in the group of people who were reluctant to do anything more than research and send email from my computer, and I would not have dreamed of using a credit card over the Internet. My view of what was going on in the online world at that time was that it was intended strictly for education and research and entertainment with the games that were being developed.

During the time period between 2001 and 2003 the Internet again took a jump as blogs and other self-published content became more commonplace. I was teaching technology at a middle school during this time, so I began teaching the students how to write some basic HTML code to set up one page sites on the web. We had great fun setting up these sites, and the parents enjoyed seeing what we were doing. Many of my parents at that time were small business owners, and I often wonder today if they had more vision and insight into the possibilities of what we were doing in the classroom and in the computer lab back then than I did.

Our computer lab at the school consisted of fifteen Apply IIC computers with either 3.5" or 5 ¼" floppy disks. The floppy disks were the ones made from a strong polyester film material called Mylar. We were all networked together and share one printer. Looking back at this time I realize that it was amazing that my school even had something as advanced as this for the students to take advantage of and learn from.

It seemed like overnight we were all using the search engines like Alta Vista and Lycos to find out everything from movie show times and map locations to medical information and more. Soon Google became the search engine of choice and the others started to fall by the wayside. It wasn't until 2005 that I became aware of people setting up one page websites for the purpose of selling information to others, and I knew then that everything was about to change.

The very first site I saw that utilized this type of online marketing strategy was one that sold an eBook on how to write a eulogy. This eBook sold for about twenty dollars and helped people who had been asked to give a eulogy at a funeral for a loved one who had passed. This was when I made the decision to come online to serve people who needed my help. Even though I wasn't sure exactly what I had to offer, it was my belief that I could learn how to do this and make a good living in the process.

I believe everyone should make the effort to become an entrepreneur of sorts. By this I mean that it simply isn't healthy or natural for adults to be enslaved to an employer or a company during their entire working life. Don't get me wrong; I think that everyone benefits from working for someone else for a period of time when they are young. This builds character and gives you a renewed appreciation for having your own business later on. But having a company dictate your every move is not good for you or for your family members.

Growing up I had many friends who came and went because their fathers were transferred to a new city by the companies that employed them. Typically the man left first, and that left the wife and kids to pack up the house, say goodbye to friends, and move on to the new location. This was a heartbreaking process for everyone involved, yet very few people did anything about it.

There were a few exceptions to this. While I was living in Miami, Florida as a young teenager, I had a close friend named

Cathy. Cathy and I were very good friends and had much in common. In fact, she and I started a babysitting service the summer I turned twelve years old. We did extremely well with this business. But I digress. This is really about Cathy's father, Tom. It was just the two of them, and even though she and I were very close I never asked Cathy about what had happened to her mother. I guess I thought that she had passed away long ago and she didn't want to talk about it with me. Finally, one evening during the summer when we were all sitting outside, Tom shared the details with my mother and I and a few of the other neighbors.

Tom and his family had lived in New York before moving to Miami when Cathy was eight years old. Tom was a middle management employee for a large manufacturing company, and they had transferred him to four different states since Cathy had been born. Each transfer had meant a promotion and a substantial pay raise, and Cathy's mother, a woman named Judy, was very happy about this.

When Cathy had been about to start in the third grade Tom's company again decided to send him to a new location. But Tom had had enough of this and wanted to stay put until Cathy finished elementary school. He refused to go, the company fired him, and Cathy's mother filed for divorce. Tom was given full custody of Cathy, something very rare during the 1960s, and he decided to move to south Florida where the weather was good and the cost of living more affordable than it was in New York. He took a job at a small local company so they would have enough money on which to live.

This memory was forever engrained in my mind. As a thirteen year old I connected the idea of corporate success with divorce and family mayhem.

Why Everyone Should Have A Job In The Very Beginning

Having a job when you're trying to start your own business can be both positive and negative. I still have some mixed feelings about this. Working for someone else can be crucial to your success in the long run. In fact, I believe that everyone should work as an employee for at least a year in their young adult life in order to appreciate what that means and requires from you as an individual. Then you can go on to work in a family business or start your own business as an entrepreneur with your new perspective.

The problem that arises is that many people become comfortable in their job over time. This can mean that you no longer have the ambition and the drive to do what it will take to start your own business. This happened to me for many years when I worked as a classroom teacher. I loved working with the children and knew that I would receive a paycheck for the same amount once a month as long as I kept teaching. This made me complacent when it came to taking the time necessary to doing something on my own. I had my real estate business during all of the years I was teaching, but real estate is cyclical and I never went out of my way to pick up new clients. It wasn't until the situation at work became unbearable that I was again ready to go after my own dream of working from home on my computer.

Look closely at your present situation. With the economy in full recovery at this point it may be tempting for you to stay at your job and make the best of it. Think about the way that you are justifying and rationalizing this action. When I finally did this it was amazing to me the story I had created about why I had to stay working as an employee instead of leaving that false sense of security behind to fulfill my own hopes and dreams.

If you have been out of work for six months or a year, or perhaps even longer, you may be thinking that this is the best time to find a new job and start working again. I would encourage you to do this only if you are strapped for cash, and even then to only do it temporarily while starting your own business online. Becoming unemployable was the best thing that ever happened to me.

A job is never a certainty. So many events can occur that will be beyond your control over time, and you may have even heard stories about companies that go under without much notice to their employees or the creditors. We have all heard the stories of people who worked for twenty years or more at a company and were then let go, long before they could receive the financial incentives and benefits they had counted on for their entire adult lives. You deserve more than to be put in this position after giving any company the best years of your life.

Start a small business online just to get a foothold into the world I am describing here. Once you see that you can earn even a small amount of money as an online entrepreneur you will be convinced that you have more control over your own life that you ever thought possible. By moving slowly you will be able to incorporate these ideas into your thinking and make the best possible decisions as to what is best for you and your family.

Have You Become Too Comfortable In Your Job?

I spoke about this earlier, and now I want to go into even more depth as we explore this idea. Are you too comfortable at your job to become a successful entrepreneur? If you stop to think about the job you are currently working at you may discover that you have become complacent about starting and building your own business because your job provides a steady paycheck to pay your monthly bills and expenses. This can be dangerous!

I worked as a classroom teacher for twenty years. Every month I received a paycheck that I used to make my house payment, car payment, and to cover my other expenses. It wasn't until I had cancer for the first time and was not able to work for six months that I realized just how much that job was costing me. It's just so easy to get caught up in the day to day life situations that require so much time and energy we can't possibly think of taking on something new.

At the same time I was teaching I was also working in real estate as a listing broker and residential appraiser. Once I could not teach this became my only income. This real estate work allowed me to make my own hours, set my own appointments, and have control over the amount of income I could earn. If it had not been for my ability to make money in real estate while I was undergoing treatment for my cancer, I would surely have lost my home and had to file for bankruptcy.

Instead, I had a steady flow of income coming in and was able to meet all of my financial obligations. Even though I was in physical pain and had to reschedule my appointments many times, I knew that I could get the work done by the end of the week and receive payment for what I had completed. This gave me peace of mind in a way I cannot fully describe. One of the problems with this was that real estate goes in cycles, and sometimes you have a year or longer where you earn very little money, while my teaching job continued to provide me with a steady paycheck no matter what was transpiring in the world's economy.

How can you avoid being caught up in what I call the 'paycheck comfort zone'? Ask yourself some serious questions to see where you are in this process. Are you satisfied with the number on your paycheck? Are you alright with the amount of time and effort required to stay at your job? If you or a family member were to become ill, if you'd want to relocate to another city to live, or to want to take time off to pursue other interests, would your job accommodate you? Is the amount of money you earn at your job sufficient for what you need in your life?

All too often, some of us also get attached to old jobs that feel extremely comfortable. For example:

Dexter took a job as a bartender after he dropped out of school and couldn't get a job. He made good tips and now he's still doing the same job. He's got a lot of outside interests – he's also an artist – so he's kind of let his day job go by.

Anita had been a corporate executive for a dozen years. When she moved to a new city for family reasons, she accepted a job as a teller in a small bank. She can't move up and she can't move on and still remain in the same town. She's starting to get restless, and her boss is wondering why she's still working there.

Stanley started a business as a life coach. He wasn't very successful at this and looked for more options. He accepted an online job that fell into his lap, where he developed online training programs for a medium-sized company. The work was easy and fun. Originally Stanley figured he'd use the money from this job to support his business with technology and assistants, but he soon got very comfortable. His salary began to feel like an allowance or veterans benefit.

These examples are composites and they're pretty extreme. But many of us fall into patterns that lead to career lethargy.

What's the problem? Well, when you're treading water at the local creek, you don't develop skills in competitive swimming. You get comfortable. And then you reach a point where you can't make a comeback. Your energy – both physical and mental- operates on a different wavelength.

There's almost always a way to change careers, but you have to start as soon as possible. By way of analogy, if you haven't worked out in five years, you probably need to start with a trainer. You need some powerful external motivation to start or else you need to find some way to get rewarded for your initial efforts. This is why becoming an online entrepreneur, by starting out as a weekend marketer, is so appealing.

What If We Become Weekend Marketers™?

There is a certain mindset that goes along with taking the leap from being an employee to becoming an entrepreneur. As an employee you look to your boss to find out what the company wants to do next; as an entrepreneur *you* make the decisions as to what actions and steps you will take to move forward. If it's going to happen, it is entirely up to you to see it through from inception to fruition. You must have the inner strength to trust your intuition and gut instincts when it comes to making smart decisions, both in life and in business. This requires you to have the self confidence to know you can achieve your goals.

This is what I wrote about in my recent book, *The Inner Game of Internet Marketing*, and it applies to other areas of your life as well. You can do it, and quitting your job when it's right for you to become an online entrepreneur will change your life forever.

You must first do the work of looking deep inside to decide exactly what type of lifestyle would make you happy. This may take some time, so make a serious effort to determine what your next steps should be.

Are you living the lifestyle that suits your personality and interests? Most of us went to school to learn how to do something we could get a job doing in order to earn enough money to live.

Other times we pursue a career path based on our family's ideas of what would be the most suitable career path.

For me, I started out by wanting to be a veterinarian because I love animals, but ended up realizing that it was just too difficult for me to see the pain and suffering of the sick and injured animals that are brought in to the vet's office each day. Instead, I made the decision to work at something else and have animals at home as my pets. I always have a small menagerie at my house, consisting of dogs, cats, and sometimes even a few reptiles.

I learned to sell real estate while I was still in my early 20s, and a few years later to become a residential appraiser. I truly enjoyed both of these activities and was self-employed for a number of years. When I wanted a more rewarding career I returned to school at the age of thirty to earn my teaching credential. There was a shortage of teachers at that time so I was able to become employed as a classroom teacher right away, something I also enjoyed doing for many years.

It wasn't until I turned fifty years old that I realized I had very little say over my lifestyle and my financial independence. Each day I was up by four-thirty and out the door well before six in the morning. I was completely at the whim of the economy, the lenders, and the school district when it came to decisions about my work. I had lived through a strike when the union and the school district could not agree on a number of issues, and through two major recessions when interest rates on home loans went through the roof.

These days I make my own hours and plan my days to include the activities I most value. We each have interests, beliefs, and values that we wish to pursue, and having the time to do this is a unique gift most people will not experience until they retire some day.

You may want to spend time:

- Homeschooling your children or grandchildren

- Volunteering in your community

- Pursuing religious or spiritual studies

- Engaging in a health and fitness regime

Another part of the entrepreneurial equation is that you will actually save money by working from home.

- I spend about one fourth of what I used to on gasoline for my car because I don't drive very many miles any longer

- I'm able to shop at the farmer's market on Thursday afternoon and spend time choosing my produce

- I enjoy a movie every couple of weeks, and go to the afternoon matinees both to save money and get out while it is still daylight

- My pets get the royal treatment at a discount price because of the Wednesday afternoon vaccination clinic and grooming salon at my veterinarian's office

- I receive a 10% Tuesday morning discount at some of my local retail stores because I am over 55

I believe that becoming an entrepreneur, at least on a part-time basis to begin with, is the solution to the dilemma I have been describing here. You can get started online very inexpensively, and then make the decision if you would like to take it further and leave your job in the future. You owe it to yourself to see if this would be a better fit for your personality, interests, and family situation than to continue working at a job that is so confining.

What Day Is It Today?

Working online gives you such great freedom that you may find yourself mistaking one day for another. I seem to always get Monday and Tuesday confused. By Wednesday I'm usually all straightened out because that's when I go to my Rotary Club meeting. Then I mix up Friday and Saturday later in the week.

I now say that every day is Thursday in my world. That's due to the fact that I think of Thursday as an uneventful day where I can do as I please without being rushed.

Observing Human Behavior

This year I was invited to an adult Easter egg hunt by some people I have recently come to know. They are successful entrepreneurs whose children also own businesses.

The couple hosting the event had obviously spent lots of time and effort to make sure all of the eggs were well hidden on their property. With over an acre of land at their disposal it was possible for them to utilize the outside of their house, the pool, the barn, and the grounds to do this right.

I knew about the egg hunt when I accepted the invitation to attend. Anticipating that I would be out in the yard I wore my older black shoes and pants, instead of my shiny new brown patent leather ones and a long flowered skirt. I thought that this was good preparation for what would occur that day. They served a delicious brunch when I arrived, allowing for people to show up and eat after they finished with church services or anything else they might need to do on Easter morning. It turned out I only knew about half of the people who had been invited, so I introduced myself to each person as they came into the house.

It was so interesting to watch and observe the behavior of the people participating in this event. The people moved themselves into three groups as the egg hunt got underway, without anyone giving more specific directions.

The couple's adult children got busy right away, sweeping the area without saying a word to anyone else. They also did not check on what the others were doing until after they had each gathered several eggs. They seemed to have some strategy in place as they moved about, and they always seemed to find another egg in an area where others had already looked. They are all entrepreneurs and I call them the 'achievers'.

Another group of people started complaining very quickly about it being 'too hard' to find the eggs. They kept asking the couple to give them some hints and to tell them if they were 'hot' or 'cold' as they searched. They also tended to stay much closer to the main house during the search and watched the others to see what they were doing. I found out later that this group was composed primarily of supervisors and middle management employees. I refer to them as the 'workers'.

I was among the third group of people, and I dubbed these as the 'thinkers'. This group tended to move very slowly and methodically around the property, and was much more willing to get dirty. They moved things about, such as taking the door off of an area where the pool cleaning equipment was stored and turning over large stepping stones in the garden. They also walked to every corner of the property in search of hiding places that might not be visible from a different vantage point. They found lots of eggs, but not nearly as many or as quickly as did the first group, composed of entrepreneurs.

I was fascinated with this experience. I came to the conclusion that entrepreneurs – the 'achievers' - work quickly to achieve success with what they are working on, forming ideas and strategies as they go. If something does not work out, they simply turn their focus and attention to something else that may work.

The group of employees – the 'workers' - was stuck in the place of expecting someone else to hold their hand and guide them to the correct answer. These people are very smart, but they do not think for themselves very well.

The third group – the 'thinkers' -, where I ended up at the time, was willing to explore and think 'outside of the box' for the most part, but they wasted precious time by insisting on being so thorough. I saw that as perfectionism, which can cost you dearly in the long run. In the time it takes to uncover every possibility, others have flown past you and achieved their goals.

I'd like to think that I would be among the 'achievers' if I were to be invited to this event again in the future. I would quickly make the decision about where to look, form a strategy to get started, and then work quickly to meet my goal as quickly as possible.

Fitting In

Many of us were raised to be conformists. Even if you came from a creative or artistic family you probably realized from a very young age that it's much easier to 'fit in' than to show the outside world your individuality. And if you went to public schools in the United States, any creativity or uniqueness was crushed, or at least discouraged, very quickly.

Towards the end of my public school teaching career in Los Angeles, around 2004, I found myself in a meeting with some administrators and policy personnel. I was describing a project I wanted to do with my fifth grade class. One of the administrators turned to me and asked,

"Who do you think you're teaching here?"

My answer came quickly.

"I'm teaching creative thinkers who will be the leaders of tomorrow."

I'll never forget what happened next. He leaned in close and pointed his index finger right in my face. Then he raised his voice so everyone in the back of the room could hear him and he said,

"No, you're not. You are teaching average children. These are average or below average kids, the kids of immigrants, who will do as they are told and become hard-working, obedient employees in the future and a benefit to our society as a whole."

At that very moment my teaching career ended, at least in my mind. It would be two more years before I could officially resign, but I no longer believed in what I was doing. I was one of the obedient employees he was talking about, so I went to work each day, did as I was told, and made it as pleasant as possible for the children with whom I had daily contact. But my dream of teaching in a way that would foster greatness had been crushed and I saw that there was absolutely nothing I could do to change the circumstances. Two years later I had resigned my position as a teacher with the public school system.

This Isn't For Everyone

That's right; even though I believe that everyone should become an entrepreneur, the entrepreneurial lifestyle is not right for everyone. If what I am describing here does not appeal to you, then modify it to make it fit your needs and desires.

You may be in a job or career that meets your needs. In fact, you may actually look forward to getting up and going to work each morning. I have many friends who feel this way. I even felt this way for the first five to ten years of my twenty year classroom teaching career.

I could not wait to jump out of bed each morning and get ready to go to school. My car was filled with the materials I would use to teach my lessons on science, math, language arts, social studies, and more.

Then it all began to change. The first change occurred in 1992 when I was diagnosed with breast cancer. My life grinded to a halt as I underwent a radical mastectomy, radiation treatments, and chemotherapy. As if all this was not enough to endure, I soon began to learn about the financial ramifications of having a life threatening illness while you are an employee.

It turned out that I had accrued almost fifty days worth of sick pay over the five years I had been working as a teacher. This meant that I would receive my full pay for the next ten weeks, while I was going through the operations and treatment required to save my life. Then I received twenty days of half-pay, so for the following four weeks I was paid half of what I had been earning as a full-time employee with the school district.

After that I would only receive money based on any insurance I may have taken out previously that would cover me for this type of event. I was thirty-seven years old at this time, so I did not have that type of extended coverage because I had not yet anticipated the need for it. Several years later the school district implemented a program where other teachers could donate their accrued sick days to someone who was caught up in this type of situation, but at the time it was not available to help me. Years later, when I resigned, I made sure to donate all of my remaining sick days to others who could use them in the future.

Just when I thought it couldn't get any worse, it did. The school I had been working at since the very beginning of my teaching career sent me a letter that crushed me. Because I had not been actively working for the past six months they had replaced me with another teacher. When I was ready to return to work without any medical restrictions I would be placed at another school within the Los Angeles School District.

I had no say in this decision. The school district is a business like any other, and they make decisions based on the needs of their business. This is what can happen to you as an employee, when your daily life can be affected by decisions made by people you will never even meet face to face.

This was difficult both psychologically and financially. As soon as I felt better I began to do real estate appraisals again. The mornings were tough for me, but I felt good by about noon each day. I scheduled my appointments in the afternoons and only took assignments no more than an hour's drive from my house. I was earning money, getting out among people, and feeling productive once again after a long hiatus. I was also earning money, and this felt fantastic. When I was out working each day I did not feel like a cancer patient.

This should have turned on a light bulb in my brain to tell me that having a business had valuable benefits over that of working as an employee, but it would take me many more years to come to that realization.

Some Thoughts on Entrepreneurship

I am an entrepreneur. Just the sound of that makes me feel like I'm on top of the world. What do you think of when you hear that word - entrepreneur? Do you have visions of sleeping in every morning, traveling the world, and enjoying financial freedom? Or, does it conjure up thoughts of sleepless nights, an uncertain future, and no stability for your family? Changing your perspective on this may change your life and increase your bottom line in a way you have never before imagined.

I had always thought I understood its meaning, but when I came online in 2006 I realized I had no idea at all what being an entrepreneur truly entailed.

Entrepreneurship is the word that perfectly describes what we do when we create an online business. An official definition is *'one who organizes a business venture and assumes the risk for it.'* I take that to mean that an entrepreneur assumes full responsibility for whatever may happen in their business, and takes regular action to ensure that the business thrives on a daily basis.

As a child I had been quite entrepreneurial. When I was twelve years old two friends and I (my first JV partners) started a babysitting service for the summer. I mentioned one of these girls, Cathy, earlier in this book. The other girl was Mary Ann, the child of immigrant parents who encouraged her to think for herself. Cathy, Mary Ann, and I had lofty goals for our new business venture. Our goal was to earn enough money to buy our own school clothes for the next year, and to buy new bicycles as well.

We knew we could not do this alone, so we found other girls to help us and put them into teams of two to babysit for the people we could not serve due to overlapping schedules. We did this all summer long and earned quite a bit of money, at least according to our standards at the time. We each met our goal and had enough money to buy our own school clothes that fall, new bicycles, and even had spending money left over. That was also my first experience with outsourcing. Lots of girls came to us for work that summer, and my friends and I earned 10% of everything they earned by helping us in our business because it was too much for us to handle on our own.

The most important part of this experience was learning how to run a small business, feeling confident in doing so, and working with partners in order to achieve a goal.

My Real Estate Career

I had always thought of myself as an entrepreneur during my previous adult life. I worked as a real estate broker and residential real estate appraiser in California for twenty years before coming online to start my business in 2006. But once I started my Internet business I realized that I had not been an entrepreneur at all in my previous life. It turned out that I was self-employed in my real estate business. Being an entrepreneur and owning your job as a self-employed person are two very different things.

In the world of real estate I was simply following a prescribed course of action by fulfilling my duties as an appraiser or working as a broker in helping people to buy or sell property. There was little originality or creativity in this, as I was required by state law to adhere to the strict rules and regulations set forth in the real estate code. My assignments came from attorneys, Certified Public Accountants, private individuals, lenders, and mortgage brokers. I completed my assignments in a timely manner and was paid for the work I had completed.

Looking back I was able to see that I simply 'owned' a job that was lucrative when the economy was on an upswing and dismal when the economy was in a downturn. If I had been working in real estate full time I could have taken actions to ensure a more steady flow of work and revenue over the years, but doing it piecemeal did not allow me that freedom.

Entrepreneurs Call The Shots

Now that I am an online entrepreneur, I call the shots. Yes, there are many risks associated with my business, but I am more concerned with the experience of living my life to the fullest and having an impact on the world than I am with possibly making a decision that will not work out the way I had planned. Every day takes me further from my comfort zone and stretches me as a human being. Instead of receiving a predictable paycheck on a regular basis, I have the opportunity to create both wealth and satisfaction in my life.

When I wake up each morning I am ready for work. I may not get started until later in the day, but I am the person in charge and I make that decision. This means that I am totally and completely responsible for what happens in my business. This is a feeling that empowers me to do my very best. If it's going to happen, it must begin with me taking action. I absolutely love what I do, so waking up at work is a joyous state of mind for me to be in on a regular basis.

Sometimes I decide to create a new product and begin my work on that. Other times I am recommending affiliate products. At least once a year I am busy writing another book. Content creation, online visibility, and ongoing credibility are my focus each day, and it's completely up to me to succeed with this to reach and surpass my personal and professional goals.

This also means that I have no commute, no boss, and no co-workers. I used to leave my house before six o'clock each morning, drive several hours throughout the day to get to my various destinations, and not have much input as to where I would be driving to so that I could conduct my real estate business profitably. I also worked as a classroom teacher during this time, so I had to deal with several administrators, other teachers, and support staff, many of whom were not very pleasant to be around.

That meant that I was both an employee and self-employed for more than twenty years. These were two different worlds with almost no overlap. Now that I am an entrepreneur I only spend time with the people whom I choose to interact with, whether that is independent contractors who are helping me, my prospects, or my clients.

Making the mental shift from employee or small business owner to entrepreneur is one that comes easier to some people than to others. I believe that you must make a mental shift if you are considering becoming an entrepreneur. If you are going to do this online, as I highly recommend that you do, then your shift will be even more dramatic as you determine how you wish to live your life without having to spend time each day at an office or other work location.

I love working from home, or from wherever I happen to be at the moment. I've managed my business from cities across the United States, Canada, throughout Europe and Asia, and even from aboard a cruise ship on several occasions!

Are You One Of The 3%?

It turns out that only about 3% of the population at any given time is cut out for the rigors the life of the entrepreneur must endure. Are you one of the 3%? I have people come to me on a regular basis to learn how to start an online business. It is my feeling and belief that many of them do not succeed due to the fact that they just don't realize what goes into being an online entrepreneur. Most of them have a background similar to mine, where they were either an employee for many years or self-employed in a career. Becoming an entrepreneur is hard work, and you must wear many hats during your first year before you can outsource any of the required tasks to others. It's best if you have some idea of what needs to be done before turning it over to someone else.

According to my research on the topic of entrepreneurship, people aged forty-five and older are those most likely to become entrepreneurs. They do this for both financial and personal reasons. They are also more likely to have been successful in a previous job or a career for at least ten years before deciding to start their own business.

Creativity, Leadership, and Innovation As An Entrepreneur

My belief is that being an entrepreneur requires varying amounts of leadership, innovation, and creativity. Now before you throw in the towel and decide this is more than you bargained for, I'll share with you that I used to think of myself as the least creative person in the world. I thought of creativity as manifesting itself in art, music, and language, and these were not my strengths. Instead, I considered myself to be more of a left-brain thinker. Now I create products and courses and write articles and books, and have never been so creative in my life. So, as you can see, everything is relative to where you are along the continuum of life.

As far as leadership, there were very few times I felt like a leader before starting my online business. During my years of working as a teacher I was the leader in the classroom each day. But when it came to being a leader among my peers, those experiences were few and far between. I simply did not have the confidence to stand up and say what I thought about most issues. So many opportunities passed me by because I felt that someone else would do a better job than I ever could. Now it's totally different. I have gone on record as someone who says what she thinks and shows others how to get started with a profitable online business. I host teleseminars and webinars for people from around the world who look to me for help with their business strategy. Standing up for myself and for those who come to me for help and advice is part of who I am these days.

Innovation is something that I was not familiar with until I came online and started my real business education and learning. I'm not sure that word was ever mentioned while I was a classroom teacher or in the world of real estate, or at least I was not aware of any discussion on this topic. Now I am surrounded by innovators who are changing the way we do business on the Internet. I am proud to say that some of these people are my friends, and I find it is very exciting to watch them and to be a part of this type of inspired action. I've learned that you don't have to be an innovator yourself to take advantage of the miraculous changes that are coming about in the world of online marketing.

How Do You Get Started As A Weekend Marketer?

"You can do anything you set your mind to do."

Those are very powerful words. My mother said them to me, in one way or another, hundreds of times as I was growing up, but I didn't understand completely what she meant by this at the time. It wasn't until I made the decision to start my own business on the Internet that her words rang true with me. I am just grateful that she lived long enough to see the success and joy I achieved from being an entrepreneur, and to hold my first book in her hands so she could better relate to what I was working to achieve. She showed off that book to everyone she encountered during those last two years of her life.

You can achieve the success you want in your life by simply changing your thinking and your perspective in regards to the world around you. You already have the ability, so all you need to do is focus on your most valuable ideas and ask for help to implement these ideas into something tangible. Taking action is the key to success with all of this. The possibilities are unlimited and your online business can look like whatever would work for you.

Are you willing to do this? You may well be one of the 3% of the world's population I talked about earlier who is truly cut out to be an entrepreneur. If you're still excited about this after reading my story then you owe it to yourself to get started. Make the decision to take personal responsibility for what you want to achieve, and spend some time each day thinking creatively about how you want to begin. It will take relentless persistence, but you can achieve all of your goals and dreams.

The Beginning of Your
Weekend Marketer™ Journey

Once you get started with the Weekend Marketer™ program in the next section of this book your life will change in some amazing ways. You'll be learning new terminology you may never have heard before. Just to give you a taste of what's to come, here are some things to think about as you embark on your own entrepreneurial journey:

1. Focus on what you can do today to get started. Instead of worrying about something that may or may not occur in the future, take action on what you know how to do right now. Too many people spend months writing a sales letter, completing an eBook, or trying to master some new technology instead of just starting to blog and finding products and services to promote. This will get your cash flow moving and give you the time to perfect other aspects of your business over time. For every activity you engage in, ask yourself if this will lead to income in the very near future. If not, move on to something more productive.

    Action Step: Make a list of what you need to do this week. Now cross off everything that is not directly related to making money. Next, cross off everything you do not know how to do and find someone you can delegate those tasks to. The things that should be left on your list are ones like blogging, writing articles to submit to the directories, and finding an appropriate affiliate offer to send to your list, once you start building one. Content creation and marketing become the highest valued activities you will engage in every day.

2. Remember that building your list is a crucial part of this process. In the offline world a list is referred to as a customer database, and it is just as important online. It's virtually impossible to earn six figures a year or more unless you have your own responsive list. I have branded myself as someone who can make huge profits with a tiny list, but list building is still top of mind with me on a daily basis. I build my list with keyword rich blog posts, article marketing, social media, teleseminars, and joint ventures (JVs), just to name a few methods. I also use my 'channels' for list building, and these include YouTube, Amazon, and iTunes.

Action Step: Send an email to your list, if you have one, and ask them what type of information they would like to receive from you. Start emailing them at least twice a week to get them to be more responsive to what you are sharing. If you do not yet have a list of prospects, keep reading and know that I will explain all of this is great detail in later sections of this book.

3. Don't allow yourself to get caught up with the 'bright, shiny object' syndrome. Even I can get distracted by the latest and greatest new Wordpress plugin, an advanced application, or a training course on something that sounds very interesting. Remember to stay on course and you will achieve success much more quickly. Going off on tangents leads to frustration and overwhelm, two of the most powerful enemies of the entrepreneur.

   Action Step: Look to see what you have purchased during the past thirty days. Go through every bit of each product or course before buying anything else. This is a bit like going shopping in your own closet to see what you already own and can use right now, except that everything on your hard drive fits you well and is the perfect color!

4. Make a time commitment to your online business. While I was a 'weekend marketer' I dedicated ten to fifteen hours a week to my online business. Once I was working online full time I dedicated forty hours a week to building everything up and maintained that level of commitment for a full year until I finally was able to cut down my weekly working hours. I had been working many more hours than that while I was a classroom teacher and working in real estate, so it just made sense for me to be just as dedicated on the Internet to get my

business up and running. You need time each day to work on your daily tasks, as well as time to learn now things that will help to build your business in the future.

Action Step: Take out a calendar and mark off time each week to work on building your business. Be willing to give up activities that will not bring you closer to your goals.

Develop Your Signature Brand

You need to establish your credibility in order to build a successful online business. The best way to do this within the shortest amount of time is to create a signature brand that people will get to know, like, and trust over time. The people you want to reach are the ones in your target market so that you can turn them into prospects and clients. With solo entrepreneurs, which most of us are at the beginning of our entrepreneurial journey, we are the brand. This means that you want to get your name and face everywhere as quickly as possible.

Start with a signature site that tells people who you are and what you do. We use Wordpress for this because of the ease of use and flexibility of this platform. You may want to have a logo designed, using the colors you will be branding and a professional photograph of yourself. This site must clearly and adequately explain who you are, what you do, and how you can help the people who visit to achieve their goals. I recommend using a sticky post that will remain at the top of your site all of the time. This post will be similar to the information on your site's 'About Page' in that you will explain who you are and what you do. This gives visitors a way to understand how you will be able to help them in the future.

The next step in this process is to create a free giveaway for visitors to your site who choose to join your list. This giveaway, in the form of a short report, must be *at least* as good as anything you would sell to someone. Take your time in creating this, and include as much valuable and usable information as possible so that you continue to establish your credibility as each new prospect reads your report. I think of this as a way to build your reputation and credibility one person at a time. Do not worry about it being perfect; later on you can always come back and edit or revamp it completely.

Create a signature presentation on your topic that can be delivered both online and in person. This will further establish you as an expert as you become a sought after presenter. I started by practicing a fifteen minute talk I could present at my Rotary Club. I then expanded that to a ninety minute PowerPoint presentation that I've now given at live events across the country and beyond.

Finally, create a product based on your signature brand. You can use the information contained in your free giveaway as well as that included in your presentation as the basis of an outline for your product. The result will be a product that will turn your prospects into clients.

It is possible to brand yourself as an expert in your field very quickly by taking the time to develop your signature brand and following through with your online business plan.

The Season Of Excuses

As I continue to work with people in the area of building a profitable business, I hear the same excuses over and over. Some of the more memorable ones are:

"But you don't understand. My business is DIFFERENT."

"Sure, that works for you, but I'm new to all of this."

"I'm too old." "I'm too young." "I'm too..."

"I'm on (insert guru's name here) list, and they said I should try (insert name of latest product or service here)."

And my all-time favorite:

"I can't afford a mentor."

When I started my serious exercise and eating plan at the first part of this year I soon realized that I was making the exact same excuses! Even though I was showing up at the gym each week, I found myself telling the trainers that they did not understand why I wasn't making much progress because my body was different.

As I observed others losing weight and replacing fat with muscle I justified this to myself by thinking that it was working for them, but not for me, because I was new and needed time to settle in to the exercise and fitness routines they were teaching me. I also told them that I was too old to be able to make the kind of progress some of the others were making.

I soon began searching the Internet for help and found myself telling the trainers at my gym that people online were recommending an entirely different regime that I was going to check out. When they recommended that I work out privately with a trainer three times each week I told them that it was just too expensive for my budget.

I had effectively taken myself out of the game and ensured my failure by not trusting them to guide me in the right direction. When I finally realized this I apologized profusely and began to make a serious and consistent effort to follow exactly what they were recommending. The result was that I began to lose weight, increase my muscle mass, decrease my BMI (Body Mass Index), and feel better overall.

Once I stopped making excuses and started focusing on how to do the best I could under the guidance and direction of those I trusted, everything changed overnight.

Have you been guilty of making similar excuses in your life? If so, move past that way of thinking and be open to the changes and possibilities that are waiting for you on the other side.

Over the past six years, during which time I have become a successful online entrepreneur after transitioning away from being an employee and small business owner, I have come up with my own *Principles of Entrepreneurial Success*. I'll share these with you, along with some concrete examples of how they have come to be a part of the person I am today. Always remember that you are a work in progress, and someone who is in the process of becoming the person you would like to be.

Principles of Entrepreneurial Success

1. Living in Integrity - Integrity is about much more than honesty. In fact, living in integrity involves being true to yourself as much as being true to other people around you.

I lived the first half of my life out of integrity for much of the time. Everything I did, every action I took and interaction I had with another person, was based on me feeling like I was not equal to them. When I became an entrepreneur I began living my truth, which is based on the premise that I have just as much to offer others as they do me. This brought about a shift in my thinking that continues to serve me well all these years later.

2. Self-Confidence – It wasn't until I was well into my thirties that I realized just how low my self-esteem was and that I lacked self-confidence in almost every area of my life. This realization led me on a path of self discovery that made me even more confused. After a few years of extensive reading and attending seminars to explore the reasons why I felt as I did, I finally decided to just let it go and get on with my life. I think of my life today as one where I am the master of all that happens and the outcomes of my behavior and actions. This is not an 'audition'; we have one lifetime to do the things that have meaning for us.

3. Risk Taking – During my twenties and early thirties I made several real estate investments. A few of these worked out well, while others fell short of my expectations and it was all I could do to break even. During this time I came to the erroneous conclusion that the only way someone like me would be able to make great advances in the area of real estate was if I had someone older or smarter to help me, or if I could just meet someone who would mentor me to success. The truth was that I was just not willing to take the risks

associated with investing, and until I did each transaction's outcome would be like rolling the dice.

These days I take risks, albeit calculated ones, on an almost daily basis. Every time I outline an idea for a new product or course, set up a new affiliate campaign, or send a promotional email to me list, I am risking my reputation and my financial future on the outcomes of my decisions. What I particularly love about taking business risks is that this is a learnable skill, so over time my ideas and decisions have become much better than they were when I was just getting started.

4. Taking Responsibility – Poor people tend to blame others for their circumstances, while wealthy people take full responsibility for what happens in their life. It may seem like I'm making an unfair judgment and generalization here, but I am not talking about this part of life as it relates to finances at all. Instead, I am speaking of a state of mind that can keep you poor or make you wealthy once you understand the principle behind it. We must take full responsibility for everything that happens to us on a daily basis. In fact, that responsibility stretches further than just to situations you may feel that you have some control over. It's pretty easy to say that we must take responsibility for something that we say or do, but how about things that seem to happen *to* us?

What I am suggesting here is that we take responsibility for things we may feel like we have no control over in any possible way, such as an appliance breaking down at our house or an event we were looking forward to being cancelled. This is much too deep a topic for us to explore in this book, but it is a way of thinking that has shifted my thoughts and the outcomes to nearly everything I encounter in my life. As an entrepreneur this way of thinking has served me as I continue to grow as a person and as a business owner.

5. Perseverance – Sir Winston Churchill is well known for saying 'Never, never, never give up!" in regards to Britain's role in World War II. That has become one of my favorite quotes of all time, and one that resonates with my experiences working online. I have said that anyone in their right mind would have given up during the first year if their progress and performance as an online entrepreneur had been as dismal as mine, but that I had been determined to make a go of what I was learning as I saw the potential for a different way of living my life. No matter what is now thrown at me, whether it be personal or professional in nature, I understand that perseverance will pull me through to the other side, and I will be better off for having gone through whatever it was that seemed insurmountable at the time. This is how my mother and I made it through those difficult years as I was growing up, which left us homeless at one point and sleeping on the floor of a coin laundry.

6. Consistency – This is the 'tortoise and the hare' story, where the slow moving tortoise wins the race because he kept moving, while the hare raced ahead and then was too tired to see the race through to the finish line. Make an effort each and every day, no matter how small or insignificant it might seem at the time, and you will keep moving forward towards your goals.

7. Prioritizing - When you make something a priority, attention is given to it until it is completed. Make the important things in your life, such as your family and other relationships, your faith, your community, and your business a priority and they will each receive the attention that is needed so that you can achieve the level of success you want and need in order to feel fulfilled in your life's mission and vision.

8. Storytelling – Our world has evolved through storytelling, and this medium continues to be the best way to connect with other people. Do you remember listening to the adults tell stories when you were a child? That's how most of us learned our personal family history and developed a true sense of who we were growing up. As an adult, you can share stories to let people know who you are and what you stand for. I love to share stories about the charities I am involved with, people I know, and what it was like to be a classroom teacher. Each story makes a point about my life and what I believe in.

9. Goal Setting and Achieving – Growing up, and into my young adult years, I was never around anyone who talked about setting goals and then working to achieve them. The closest I ever came to this idea was when I made New Year's resolutions and then tried to remember to keep them as long as possible.

One year I made a resolution to lose twenty pounds and actually met my goal within a few months. Now I set and achieve goals regularly, and write down everything I plan to do. When I think about how different my life is now that ongoing goals are a part of it, I realize just how little chance for success I was giving myself for all of those years. If this is a new strategy for you, start out by writing down one goal in each of three areas of your life – business/financial, personal/relationships, and health/fitness – and then following through with these three goals over the next thirty days. You just might be amazed at your results.

10. Discipline – I did not grow up in a home where discipline was part of my daily life. It was just my mother and I, so we tended to be more relaxed in our habits and routine. It wasn't until I was in junior high school that I realized I may have been at a disadvantage because of this. Having structured systems and schedules in place allows for more creativity and freedom, even though this might be counterintuitive. I was used to doing things when I got around to it instead of knowing what needed to be accomplished and getting to work. Add discipline to every aspect of your life and you will be happier and more successful as you meet and surpass your goals.

11. Attitude of Gratitude – I am grateful for every moment I am alive, and thank God for his tender mercies. It is my strong belief that we should take nothing for granted. Each day is a special gift from our Creator that allows us another opportunity to serve others. Make an effort each and every day to approach your life with an attitude of gratitude and see what happens.

12. Entrepreneurial spirit – As a new online entrepreneur, I look forward to what each new day will bring. I have learned from experience that nothing happens in my business until I create something, and that is exciting and powerful. Each

day I am filled with ideas, and I must write them down or they will evaporate into thin air. Take ten minutes each day to brainstorm ideas for your business, and then make sure to look back at what you have written to decide how and when you will implement your thoughts and ideas.

"You Can Do Anything You Set Your Mind To."

To me, those are very powerful words. It really is completely up to you because you have the ability and must take action. The possibilities are truly unlimited if you take personal responsibility and focus on your life's goals as you work each day with sheer determination to live your mission and vision. Relentless persistence will expand your thinking and creativity as you walk this path.

Are You Willing To Do What It Takes?

Recently, I gave a presentation to a group of more than three hundred entrepreneurs and small business people who were working to increase their revenues and find new ways to reach their target markets. The title of my talk was 'Are You Willing To Do Whatever It Takes?' and in the ninety minutes I was on stage I shared some of my most personal experiences and how they have shaped me into the person I am today.

I told the story of how I had grown up in poverty and what that actually looked like. It was just my mother and I, and we were homeless twice before I was twelve years old. One time we had nowhere to go and ended up sleeping on the floor in a Laundromat several nights in a row.

One night, right after the bars closed, two men stumbled into the Laundromat in the darkness. My mother was on her feet within just a few moments and confronting them face to face. I had never heard the tone or the words she used with them that night, but the result was that they had turned around and left very quickly. This was the case of a mother being willing to do whatever it takes to protect her child.

I also shared what it was like to survive Hurricane Andrew in 1992. I had lived in south Florida during my teenage years, and went to school at the University of Florida at Gainesville during my freshman year. This gave me strong ties to many people there, and I used to visit them every few years.

During 1992 I had returned to Miami to spend one year living and working. I had taken a leave of absence from my teaching position and was hired by the Florida Department of Transportation as a Right-of-Way appraiser.

In August of that year hurricane season was in full swing and for the first time ever I decided to track each one on a map given out at the local grocery store. The next one was named Andrew, and as I tracked it across the Caribbean I did not realize it would cause me to lose almost all of my worldly possessions. On the morning of August 24 this Level 5 hurricane powered through my neighborhood, tearing apart everything in its wake with winds of up to one hundred seventy-five miles an hour. At the time this was the costliest natural disaster in United States history, and I feel blessed to have lived through this traumatic event.

Over the next several days my neighbors and I did whatever we had to do in order to stay alive and face the next phase of our lives.

You may not have been homeless as a child, or survived a major hurricane, but you have gone through many situations over the course of your life that have shaped you into the person you are today. Being willing to do 'whatever it takes' to make it through these trying times successfully determines the course of action you take on a daily basis. I believe each of us goes through a four level process as we encounter life's situations.

Survival, Perseverance, Mind-Shift, and Evolution

I think of our lives as being at four different levels, depending upon what we are doing, what are intentions are at the time, and what we are thinking. The first level is that of survival, whether it is literal or not. On a very basic level this is where your primal instincts take over; your need for food, shelter, and sleep. On a less dramatic level, this can take place with each new situation you encounter. The outcome of your first days at a new job or career can be based upon how well you survive.

On the first day I started working as a residential real estate appraiser I was given an assignment to go to a home, take pictures, fill out a form, and return to the office to learn how to write it all up in an acceptable way. The owner, a man named John, handed me the information on an index card. I looked at the address and thought it was about ten miles away from the office. It was just after lunch, so I told him I'd be back within two hours. He had an odd look on his face, but did not say anything.

Once I got to my car and looked up the address in my map book (this was in 1989, so we didn't 'Google' it back then) I saw that I had confused the address with a similar one, and that this house was actually about forty miles away. It was also raining pretty hard, something that seldom happens in southern California, so the round trip was likely to take more than two hours and my work at the house another hour.

I wanted this job so that I could become certified as an appraiser and have an opportunity to earn more money in less time than my other real estate work typically took me. I was in survival mode, and decided to hit the road to complete my assignment in record time, while still being safe. I did this, and upon my return to the office later that day was given a full time position for the summer.

The next level is perseverance, where you've met your basic needs and now want more from your life. I became a teacher to reach children and work with them every day as they were in the process of becoming the people they would be later on in their lives. I wanted more from my life than just surviving by working at a job; I wanted to empower young people to make a difference in their lives so they could reach their full potential and turn their dreams into reality.

As a classroom teacher I persevered by learning as much as I could so that I could continue to maximize my opportunities within the school district.

The mind shift comes next. This is actually a physical phenomenon that occurs. Where the hypothalamus and the pituitary gland meet, that's referred to as the mind-body connection. We all have many mind shifts throughout our lives, and I believe one of mine came when I made the decision to leave the work force and become an online entrepreneur. As I went through the process of resigning from the school district and closing down my real estate business for good, something changed both mentally and physically for me. It was scary at first, but once the mind-body connection was in place I saw that this was the perfect decision for my life, at the right time.

The final level is one of evolution. I am still new to this level, but I will share with you that it is quite exciting to see life from this different perspective. Many times I will slip back into perseverance level, or even to one of survival, but knowing that I have the capability of moving back up to mind-shift and on to evolution gives me the strength to keep moving and improving my life each day.

Section Two
The Weekend Marketer™

The only good jobs left are the ones where you decide what to do. We must all become entrepreneurs to prosper in this new economy.

~Seth Godin

I love this quote from Seth Godin and resonate with what he is implying. You must be open to entrepreneurship if you expect to prosper in the years ahead. Everyone must become an entrepreneur of some sort, and it may be as a weekend marketer in the very beginning. Think about what this could mean in your life, and how much time and effort you would be willing to contribute to make it all work for you and your family.

You may have heard the term 'moonlighting' in reference to someone working at a second job in order to make ends meet. This term is also used to describe someone who is pursuing their dream on a part-time basis while maintaining their 'real' job full time so they can pay their bills. Either way, the people who tend to do this are ones who have a dream they are just not willing to give up on. This dream is usually about way more than simply earning some extra money; it's about changing their life and becoming the person they feel destined to become. I have even heard people explain this phenomenon as having something inside them that needs to come out, in a way others are not able to fully understand.

What about you? What are you hoping to achieve in your life that you haven't achieved already? There had to be some deep-seeded reason that the title of this book – The Weekend Marketer™ – resonated with you on an internal level and made you want to find out more. My belief is that something stirred deep inside of you and gave you hope that what you have been dreaming of is truly possible. It is, and I am living proof of just what can be achieved if you relentlessly pursue your goal of becoming an online entrepreneur.

It all begins with the way you see yourself and the role you play in your daily life. I'm going to use a sports analogy here so that you will more fully understand what I am talking about with all of this.

You are the franchise player for your team, and you must take care of your well being in order for your team to be successful. A 'franchise player' is the one person on the team that can single-handedly lead the team to long-term success. They are typically a superior player, but need not be the best player on the team.

Like I said, this is a sports analogy, but I think it is fitting for all entrepreneurs. Your team, which consists of you and your family, must stay in optimal condition at all times. This means that you must strive for excellence, not perfection, as you build your business. Others may be more experienced, have greater talent in many areas, and be better connected with other entrepreneurs, but you can be the franchise player if you are willing to persevere, learn as much as you possibly can, and realize that this is a way of life for the long run, not for overnight or fleeting success.

You may feel that you are already an entrepreneur at heart who just stuck in a nine to five job for the time being. You can achieve great success with an online business as a 'Weekend Marketer' while you are making the transition from employee or small business owner to full time entrepreneur. I, along with tens of thousands of others, have been able to do this since the turn of the century.

When I first realized that people were doing business from their home computers in order to build online empires it was late in 2005. I was working as a classroom teacher at that time, and spending my evenings and weekends working as a real estate broker and residential appraiser. This was exhausting for me as I had become older (I had turned 50 that year) and had gone through cancer treatment and a serious work injury. As soon as I listened to a CD about setting up my own websites and earning money from home I knew I had found my calling. I could see that it would be possible for me to earn a living in a way that would highlight my skills and talents, allow me to continue being a teacher, and to give me a break from the physical stress of being away from home sixty to seventy hours a week, six or seven days each week, year in and year out.

The only problem was that I couldn't just walk away from my job and my responsibilities as well as my financial obligations. Instead, I got started right away, in November of 2005, by learning as much as I possibly could in the few hours a week I was not working or sleeping.

This meant that I spent two hours on Friday night, a time I had previously reserved for 'unwinding', usually as a zombie in front of the television set, and two hours on Saturday mornings (this had to be completed by eight o'clock so that I could get on the road to my first real estate appointment) setting up the beginnings of my online business. This continued until the following summer – 2006 - when I made the decision to quit my job as a teacher and to give away my real estate clients to others working full time in that business. By that point I realized that if I worked hard and continued to learn and implement what was working for me so far that I could easily replace my income within six months or so.

For the eight months between November of 2005 and July of 2006 I was a 'weekend marketer', and the progress I was able to make set the stage for my future as a successful online entrepreneur. Perhaps this is why I continue to enjoy getting some work done on Friday evenings and Saturday mornings, even though I no longer do any other kind of work besides my Internet business. I take off days during the week to do work in my community and to spend time with family and friends, instead of teaching or doing real estate. It's still a part of me to be a 'weekend marketer', and this has been the best decision I ever made in my life when it comes to business and lifestyle choices.

Your First Big Decision

The first decision you will want to consider is whether or not you are looking for a way to quit your job, as I was, or if you are looking for a way to supplement what you are currently doing. Or, have you been laid off or are you out of work for any other reason, such as having an injury or illness?

Many people love their job and would not want to leave before it is time to retire. I wrote my thoughts on this earlier in this book. If this describes you, then you will want to build an online business in a way that works for your present schedule so that you can begin earning some money as you build your business slowly and steadily over time.

I firmly believe that everyone, starting around the age of sixteen, should have a way to make at least some money that is not based on working for someone else or owning a business that requires trading time for money. This gives you a level of knowledge and power that will serve you well over time. Knowing that you are not completely dependent upon the economy, your company, and the decisions and actions of others for your financial needs is empowering, and something that will give you a different perspective as you go through each day.

Staying with my current job at the time, as a classroom teacher, did not apply to me because I would have needed to teach until I was sixty-eight years old in order to retire from the school district with a full pension and medical benefits because I did not begin teaching full time until I was thirty-one. I felt that my health just would not hold out for that many more years.

It would have been the year 2023 when I could have retired, meaning that I would have missed the opportunity that still exists at the current time to get in on the ground floor of the online marketing revolution. That window continues to narrow, so it's important that you jump in as soon as possible to have the best chance of success. Even though I am stating this as a fact, based on my experience, do not let me or anyone else deter you from jumping in at any time, regardless of when you are reading this book and making the decision to become an online entrepreneur.

Remember that working for someone else will always limit your income and your lifestyle choices, so if you are choosing to stay at your job you must do it for the right reasons. Having a good medical plan should not be one of them. You will be able to purchase your own medical insurance once you set up your business, and the cost will not be an issue because of your increased earning potential. I have several pre-existing conditions and am still able to pay for my own health insurance as part of an excellent group plan for business owners. Of course, you must discuss this with your family and your medical provider to find out which options are best for your short and long term needs.

If you are part of a company retirement program, schedule an appointment to sit down with the plan administrator and find out exactly what your options are. Many times it will turn out that staying at your job for five or ten more years will not be worth what you could potentially earn as an entrepreneur. This is part of the risk assessment you must discuss with your family before making any decisions that would affect them in any way.

If you want or need to completely start over due to a job loss or change of circumstances in your life, you can begin on a part-time basis during your first few months online and then ramp up your efforts to earn a full time income as soon as possible.

Phase I – Planning Your Mindset and Time Management Strategies

Get into the habit of keeping nothing on your mind. And the way to do that is not by managing time, managing information, or managing priorities. It's by managing your actions. ~ David Allen

You may have heard the saying 'If you fail to plan, you plan to fail'. When it comes to starting an Internet business this saying definitely applies. Think of this as planning for your future in a way that allows you to design the structure and outcome.

Mindset Strategies

The first step with all of this is adjusting your thinking and mindset to prepare yourself both mentally and emotionally for the changes that will occur in your life as you make this transition from whatever position you are in right now – employee, independent contractor, freelancer, or small business owner - to becoming an entrepreneur. Very quickly you will find yourself in a world where the thinking is drastically different from that of the people you have been spending time with before you initiated this change.

The idea of a mind-shift is actually a physical phenomenon that I discussed in the previous section of this book. It represents the point in our body where the hypothalamus and the pituitary gland meet and is referred to as the mind-body connection.

As a classroom teacher I was surrounded by people who were what I refer to as 'small thinkers'. They could not and would not see their lives beyond what was right in front of them. If one small part of their job was changed, such as the time they would go to lunch each day or the text book they would be using to teach a particular subject that semester, they would become angry and emotional. The complaining was overwhelming. They always thought that any changes were not fair to them, and the result of this was constant bickering among the teachers as to who was getting the shortest end of the stick at any particular time.

I can remember one year when our storage areas were reassigned. I worked at schools that were open all year around, so we were divided into four tracks. At any point in time, except for the week between Christmas and New Year's when the entire school was closed down, three tracks would be at school and one track would be on vacation. Every six or seven weeks there would be one day when the track that was going *on* vacation and the track that was returning *from* vacation would have to change classrooms. I know this sounds very confusing as I write it here, so you can only imagine how messy this was in real life.

One year the assistant principal decided to reassign the storage areas because the office needed more room for storage of their materials and paperwork. This meant that each teacher now had much less room in which to store their materials while they were 'off track'. The screaming and yelling could be heard a block away, and soon many of the teachers were in tears. You may think that I am exaggerating here for effect, but I can assure you that, if anything, I am downplaying the actual events that transpired to save space as I write.

I was teaching fifth grade that year, and my grade level was notorious for wanting to have their way all the time. I decided to offer my space to the other three 5th grade teachers because I had room at home to store my things while I was on vacation. It seemed like a kind and generous offer on my part at the time, seeing as how I would have to cart everything out of the classroom, across campus to the parking lot, pack it into my car, and then take it all out of my car at home to put it away for six weeks or so until it all had to be brought back to school and unloaded once again. However, the other teachers did not see it this way at all. They accused me of siding with the administration on this and not wanting to support them as they demanded the situation go back to the way it had been previously.

Instead of being team players and making the best of the situation, they wanted to fight about it and invest precious time and emotional energy into something that we could have dealt with on our own. I did take the time to see if there was any merit as to the accusations they were making of me, but I stood firm in my beliefs.

The point I am making here is that our time and energy are much better spent on something more positive and productive, but small thinkers will never see it this way. Businesses would go bankrupt very quickly if they chose to fight about such issues instead of becoming problem solvers that find a workable solution and then move on.

As you get away from this negative way of thinking and addressing situations that may arise in your life, you may even find yourself questioning your views in the political, economical, and world arenas. This was something that I was not expecting, but that

I have come to terms with during these past several years. I found myself doing much more listening than talking as I entered this exciting new world.

This issue of finding people to help and advise you, when everyone you know right now is either an employee or stuck in a career that requires them to trade time for money, is one that you will have to address sooner or later. I found the people I needed to spend time with by joining several non-profit organizations and learning more about charities and volunteering. These people, men and women of all ages and from various backgrounds and walks of life, opened up my eyes and my mind to a world I did not know existed. I would encourage you to seek out at least one service organization in your city and learn more about what they have to offer.

One revelation that I experienced as a new entrepreneur was that there was no longer a 'right' or 'wrong' way to do something in my business, as was the case with teaching and real estate.

In the classroom, everything I did was from a prescribed method established by the government, my local school district, and the administrators at my school. I had almost no input into the way I taught each subject, classroom discipline, and in a myriad of other areas.

When I worked as a real estate appraiser and listing broker, I had to adhere to the strict guidelines set forth by the governing bodies. I had more of a say with how these laws and rules were adopted and enforced, but that could end up being an expensive and time consuming process.

Entrepreneurs do things in a creative way that makes sense for them. You could bring a hundred entrepreneurs together and tell them your idea for a particular project and you would end up with one hundred different answers as how to best solve your problem and achieve your goals. I like this part of what I'm doing very much, as it gives me the mental freedom to expand upon my thinking of what will work.

In this initial phase of moving towards entrepreneurship you will want to think of the *Big Picture*. Make a list of your 'Why' for wanting to start an online business. This may include, but is certainly not limited to, being able to better provide for your family, getting completely out of debt, having a way to retire earlier than scheduled, purchasing a second home, being able to travel to exotic locations, and being able to volunteer your time and give to charity. All of these were a part of my 'Why', and I have not only achieved my goals but surpassed them in each of these areas as I continue my online marketing journey.

Also, write down your intentions; do you want to leave your job in order to work online, are you currently not working for any reason and need to build a business, or will you be staying at your job and pursuing your business on a part-time basis? Be prepared for the psychological impact that comes from changing your work and life, and know that you will be able to make wise decisions as they come your way.

Building Confidence

I did not realize just how low my self-esteem and confidence levels were until I made my first visit to a Rotary Club in July of 2006. I was living in a new city – Santa Clarita, California – and wanted to start volunteering some time each week as I made my transition into the world of being an online entrepreneur.

There was a Rotary group that met each Wednesday for lunch at a local restaurant, and I showed up one day to see what it was all about. I had read about Rotary on the Internet and it seemed like a group that I could connect with to get started.

When I arrived there were twenty people or so in the back room of the restaurant. As I looked around I recognized several people who had been featured in the local newspaper, including our mayor and a woman on the city council, the owners of the local radio station, my dentist, my veterinarian, and others whom I did not know. Suddenly I was overcome with a feeling of fear and inadequacy. Who was I, an unemployed former classroom teacher and real estate broker, to show up and mingle with people of this caliber? I was sure they would laugh in my face when I introduced myself. That was a defining moment in my life. I could have exited the restaurant and gone back home, or stepped forward to introduce myself. I did the latter. A woman stepped out of the group, introduced herself and shook my hand, and steered me towards the back table where I signed in as a guest. That woman, Mary Ann Colf, is still a member of our club and knows this story.

When I was introduced I did not stand up, and did not accept the microphone to say anything about myself. I just did not have the confidence to do so on that day.

Over the next few days I thought about how I had felt during that first visit to Rotary. What was I so afraid of? Why did the people in that room make me feel so inadequate and unimportant?

Two weeks later I returned to the Rotary meeting for my second visit. This time I was a little more prepared and had practiced some positive self-talk. When they handed me the microphone to introduce myself I stepped forward, made eye contact with some of the people closest to me, and said:

"My name is Connie Ragen Green and I am a former classroom teacher, real estate appraiser, and broker. I now work exclusively online, writing eBooks, creating products, and teaching online courses to people all over the world. I am happy to be here for the second time."

Even though I had earned just a few hundred dollars online at that point, I was acting 'as if' I were further along with my goals. The result was that I felt better about myself, the Rotarians were comfortable around me, and my self-confidence made a huge leap that day.

Managing Your Time

The second step is time management. As a weekend marketer you must make wise use of your time; even a thirty minute period may be used to move the business forward. You will also need some down time to think and daydream about what you want to build and create in your business.

Get used to your own company. By this I mean that you absolutely must get used to the idea of spending regular, quality time alone each day. Most of us have almost constant interruptions from the people in our life, whether these are family members, friends, or coworkers, and when we do find ourselves alone we tend to turn on the radio or television, or perhaps log on to a social media site. Starting today, allow yourself to sit quietly for thirty full minutes to gather your thoughts and let your imagination flow. This single action, indulged on a daily basis, has the power to change your life in untold ways. This is referred to as lifestyle design.

Lifestyle design is a term that first came about several years ago. There was a growing movement of people who wanted to become online entrepreneurs and make their own hours while they traveled the world. Designing your entrepreneurial life is about doing what you want to do each day, making decision based on conscious desires instead of financial need, and planning your life in such a way as to leave a legacy for your children. It's about having control over your destiny, no matter what the circumstances are in your personal life or in the global economy.

Now, let's get back to the idea of having thirty minutes of quiet, alone time each day. If you are not accustomed to doing this on a regular basis it may feel like a total and complete waste of time when you first do it. It also may seem like the time drags on, and that you could be doing many other things during the thirty minute period that would prove to be more useful and productive in building your business and getting you started on your way to becoming an entrepreneur.

You must trust me when I say that this time will pay for itself many times over, and that when you finally begin to see the value of being alone with your thoughts you will want to personally thank me for the changes that have occurred in your thinking. While you sit quietly, or go for a walk in a quiet and secluded area, your mind is free to wander. This is an activity that came naturally to use when we were young children but that was discouraged and eliminated, typically by the time we were six or seven years old, by parents, teachers, and other authority figures.

While you are alone with your thoughts and in complete solitude, think about what it will mean to have the time and financial freedom to plan each day of your life on your terms, instead of having to follow other people's schedules and ideas.

Having the time freedom to do what you want to do is extremely valuable, I'm sure you would agree. This was something I became accustomed to not being able to have a say in while I was working at jobs during my early twenties and then later on as a classroom teacher. I'll never forget the first time I missed out on a special occasion with my family. I was about twenty-five years old at the time and could not get the time off from work to attend a wedding in another state. I could have lied to my employer and called in sick, but that was not something I was going to be comfortable with. The bride and groom and most of the family understood why I couldn't attend, but it was the beginning of the realization that my life would never be my own if I continued to work for someone else.

If this has been your experience then you may already be primed for lifestyle design. It took me another twenty-five years to get there myself, but the seeds had been planted long before I took the leap and started my own business on the Internet.

The 6 Powerful Human Motivators

All people are motivated by six things. I read about this first in a personal development report published by Dennis Becker and Rachel Rofé.

They explain that if you use all six of these motivators you will be propelled to get things done, to use self-imposed deadlines, to set small daily goals, and to make constant and ongoing improvements in your systems and approaches to everything in your life.

These six motivators are:

1. *The desire to obtain power*
2. *The fear of losing power*
3. *The desire to help others*
4. *The fear of not being able to help others*
5. *The desire of achievement*
6. *The fear of not achieving*

Give each of these some thought each day this week as you spend some quiet time thinking about the ways you will be changing yourself and your daily life as you embark upon your entrepreneurial journey.

The Different Online Business Models

During Phase I of this program you will want to think about the different business models that are available to you once you get started online. Right now you are in the 'thinking' stage, so this is the perfect time to explore your options. I believe that doing this at this time will give you the best opportunity to make objective decisions and ones that come from your heart and your gut, rather than decisions that may be clouded by other people's thoughts and ideas about what is best for you.

These are some of the general areas that you will want to consider when it comes to online business models:

- Coaching – This is where you work with others, either one-one-one or in small groups, to help them to achieve their goals. I started doing this after I had been online for two years and had reached six figures a year in my own business, but there is no set requirement to be able to coach or mentor someone else. Think about the people you have paid for coaching over the years, and what qualifications you were looking for in them before you were willing to spend time and money with them.

- Information Product Creation – Creating digital information products to sell online gives you more control over your time than coaching others will. You do your research, create the product, write the sales letter, and then market it to your target audience. Your products can sell 24/7/365 while you move on to other activities. It took me a full year to create my own product, but now I can do it from start to finish in about 48 hours, proving that everything about this business becomes faster and easier over time.

- Affiliate Marketing – I made my first money as an affiliate for other people's products, and continue to earn almost half of my income in this way. As you begin to purchase products, courses, and services to help you in your own business, you will want to share them with others through your affiliate links. I know people who work exclusively in the area of affiliate marketing, and it can be quite lucrative if you focus on serving others as you recommend what you love.

- Local Business Marketing – My most successful students to date are those involved with helping small service businesses to make their phones ring. It can be very rewarding to work with local small businesses that need to get the word out about what they have to offer to people in the community. I started with a handyman and an insurance agent back in 2007, and soon others wanted me to help them as well. This is a business model that requires you to be hands-on in the very beginning, but can then be outsourced over time.

- Blogging – Even though I maintain two active blogs I do not consider myself a 'blogger' as a business model. Many people enjoy this aspect of working online and have built up quite a large following when it comes to their niched topic. You can recommend your own and affiliate products on your blog, as well as selling advertising space to others as your traffic increases over time. In some markets the bloggers have a huge say in what is going on, giving them the power to persuade and influence with their words. You can also build 'celebrity' status in your niche by blogging regularly and expressing your views.

- Amazon – Since 2011 this has been a viable business model to pursue. You must do your own writing, as

PLR (private label rights) content is no longer acceptable. I have many books available for sale on Amazon as both paperback books and books for Kindle and this has been an excellent stream of income for me. This model cannot be monetized over night, but over a few months you can become a published author and achieve best-selling status and a regular commission check each month.

- A Combination of These Business Models – My business continues to encompass a combination of these models. I enjoy the diversity of having several different business models all rolled up into one, and sometimes I work exclusively in one area, such as affiliate marketing or information product creation, for days or weeks at a time.

I certainly hope this overview has been helpful to you at this point in your process. Just knowing that there are so many choices available will give you an idea of just what is possible as a weekend marketer. I want you to believe that it IS possible to make money online and live the lifestyle you want and deserve by moving forward with your hopes and dreams.

Quitting Your Job

It may be your dream to simply walk away from your current situation and jump into the life I am describing and teaching here.

You must not quit your current job without having a plan. I am aware that I did this, but my circumstances and responsibilities made this the right choice for me at the time. The idea is to design the lifestyle you wish to live and then ease your way into it over a period of time. This way you have complete control over how this transition will occur and the effect it will have on you and the people close to you. When I made the decision to resign from my teaching job and to give away my best real estate clients it was a decision I could make without consulting anyone. If you have a spouse, partner, or dependent children they must be included in this discussion. My Mother was still alive at that time and I was helping her by supplementing her Social Security check each month, but no one else was financially dependent upon me.

Decide where you will live and how you will earn money first. I decided to move about thirty miles north of where I had been living for the previous twenty years when I began my own lifestyle design. I chose the city I relocated to, Santa Clarita, California, because I had family members close by whom I did not want to be too far away from. My Mother was almost ninety at this time and I needed to be within an hour of where she was living to visit her several times each week and help her with shopping and other errands. Within two years of coming online I was able to buy a second home in an area that had more appeal to me and now I go back and forth between the two locations. You can do the same thing.

As far as earning income, I made the conscious decision to work exclusively online. By setting up my business on the Internet I had the freedom to choose the hours I would be working each week, and what types of activities I would be involved in on a regular basis.

This meant that I did not intend to do more than a few hours each month of one-on-one coaching, and that I would only help two or three small businesses at a time with their marketing. Instead, my business was to be based on the information product model, and also with affiliate marketing.

The next step is to set up a daily schedule for yourself. I have found that the longer we have been employees the more difficult it is to adjust to the idea of being at work while we are at home. I was used to doing my real estate work from an extra bedroom, so I had some notion of what it took to be productive from home, but it wasn't until I was working from home on a full time basis that I was able to see just how distracting it can be to make your own hours.

To set up a daily work schedule that will best help you to reach your full potential, you must first make a list of the activities you need to complete on a regular basis. Then you will want to figure out which hours are your best ones each day. For example, I am most alert and productive in the morning, so that's when I tend to do most of my work. I schedule a 90 minute block of time – time blocking, also referred to as 'time boxing', is extremely effective – from around seven to eight-thirty in the morning five days a week so that I can get lots of work finished while I am at my best. Pomodoro method - I enjoy this activity so much that I will do it six or seven days a week when I am not traveling or attending a live event.

My list of regular activities also includes creating information products and courses and finding affiliate programs to recommend, so that is also on my schedule for the early morning hours of my day as well.

I have been setting goals for many years, but once I started writing them down and working to achieve them on a daily and weekly basis my life really began to turn around. Start with just three or four goals that can be in any area of your life, such as health, finances, relationships, faith, or anything else you can think of. Write each one down, along with the action steps you will take in order to achieve them by a specific date. Keep a copy of your goals next to your work area, and look at them each day to make sure that your actions are lining up with your goals. This is the key to success in this area.

You can also have minimum, target, and outstanding levels for your goals. For example, for exercise and fitness my current goal looks like this:

Minimum: Walk briskly for twenty minutes each day

Target: Walk for twenty minutes and go through my kettle bell routine for ten minutes

Outstanding: Go to the gym and take a class; do my personal program at the gym afterwards

This helps me in every area of my life to make sure I am not doing just the minimum amount of work required and to measure my progress more accurately.

Having an accountability partner or mastermind group will help you to become even more productive in all areas of your life. These are the people who listen to you while you think aloud to get their feedback. It will take some time to get going full throttle with this strategy, but once you begin to trust them to give you the best advice and suggestions, and just to hear you out, your life will begin to change. Look for someone who is at a similar level in their business as you are, instead of someone who is a year or two ahead of or behind you. This will be someone you can grow with over time and share ideas with as you give each other needed emotional support. I now have friends through my Rotary Club and other charitable organizations who have masterminded for years with others who started out around the same time as they did in their chosen careers and professions who tout this as the single most important key to their success.

These strategies will help you to build a successful and profitable business, as well as to achieve your maximum potential in all areas of your life.

Holiday Weekends

Holiday weekends can be the perfect time to make serious progress in your online business. While others are doing a variety of things, including shopping, traveling, and sitting by the pool, you can be working on something that will earn you income and build your business. I recommend starting this at the beginning of the summer and continuing all the way through the end of September.

The first time I took full advantage of a holiday weekend to further my business endeavors was Memorial Day Weekend in 2006. I knew that I would be resigning from the school district at the end of June, so I didn't have any materials to prepare for the following school year. Real estate was also very slow at this time, so I found myself with three full days to do as I pleased, except for two invitations for cook outs. I accomplished so much that weekend, including writing several articles and blog posts, speaking with a web designer about one of my sites, and going through two products I had purchased the month before to see how I could use the information they contained and if I was going to recommend them as an affiliate.

You may be thinking that you will miss all of the fun if you commit to working during the holiday weekend, but the truth is that you will enjoy yourself so much more if you feel like you are accomplishing something in your Internet business at the same time. My first working holiday weekend was a trying one, primarily because I was just getting started online and was surrounded by friends and family members who only understood the life of an employee. While they moaned and groaned about having to return to work after the long weekend was over, I just smiled and knew that I was building something that would serve me for years to come.

You must be strategic about this so that no one will feel left out and you will still be productive. I recommend working on smaller projects, such as the articles and blog posts and other things I mentioned, rather than trying to create a product or work on a book. This enables you to focus for short bursts of time and then get back to the festivities.

Make a list of small projects you will be able to work on. If you will be writing blog posts, write down the topic of the post, a few sentences of what you'd like to include, and one or two keyword phrases to concentrate on. Find a time when you can excuse yourself from the group and sit by yourself for fifteen to twenty minutes to write your post. If you do not have your computer with you, and there is not another one available for you to use, write your post in a notebook. Write as much as you can in the allotted time, and then return to the group for at least an hour. Two or three quiet sessions should be as much as you need to complete your post.

You may even want to tell the others what you are doing, and then share the results with them at the end of the day. This is an excellent way to include them in what you are doing with your business, while also making the most of the holiday weekend.

The Quarterly Getaway

I also highly recommend taking a thirty-six hour getaway every quarter. Even if you have many family and work obligations, this is doable with the help and support of your family and friends. What I am suggesting here is that once every three months you plan an overnight trip to be able to focus only on your business. When I first did this in the fall of 2006 I went to a Holiday Inn in Ventura, California. Ventura is a beautiful city along the Pacific Ocean where the mountains meet the sea. It was an hour's drive from my house and they were having a special on the room rates because it was off season. I left on a Saturday morning around seven and returned home on Sunday night around seven in the evening. During those thirty-six glorious hours I focused exclusively on creating my first product.

When I arrived that morning it was too early to check into the room, so I walked down the promenade and out onto the Ventura Pier. There were just a few people there, and the sounds of the sea gulls and the waves crashing on the beach made me feel alive. I imagined myself a successful entrepreneur who visited here regularly, something I had never thought possible in the past. I sat down on a bench and began writing my sales letter for the product I was about to create. This was my very first product, so it was a special time for me. After writing about twenty possible headlines I took off my shoes and socks and walked along the sand, letting the salt water wash up on my feet. It was cold, but I was thrilled to be having this experience.

By the time I had eaten lunch at a little place two blocks from the beach and then checked into my room, I had written about ten pages of notes and had ideas that made me feel as though there had been divine intervention. I stayed in the room until I had to check out at noon on Sunday, and my first product, a four part teleseminar series on how to write articles and blog, was ready to go.

This was at the beginning of November and I made my first sale of my own product on Thanksgiving Day, just a couple of weeks later. I knew I was on to something and continued to use the 'Quarterly Getaway' to build my business, long after I had gone full-time on the Internet.

As we complete Phase I and move on into Phase II of the Weekend Marketer™ program, I want to leave you with the idea of starting to see things differently. I'll share a story with you that further emphasizes this point.

For several years I had a medical appointment in Los Angeles every two to three months. Each time I would plan my day around getting to this appointment because of the distance from my house, the traffic, and the stress all of this caused me. I always drove the exact same way to get there, exited at the same street on the freeway, and then drove on the same surface streets until entering the front driveway of the medical office building where I needed to go. Then I would park near the front of the building and enter through the front entrance. I used the elevator to go up to the third floor and would sit in the waiting area until my name was called. I went through the exact same pattern and routine with this for years, never even thinking about changing one step in the process.

On one of my visits last year I arrived very early one time because the traffic on the freeway had been much lighter than expected. It was a warm day and I decided to walk around the building once before going inside and up to see my doctor. As I made my way towards the back of the office building I was shocked at what I found.

The back of the building was like a huge garden. There were plants and trees everywhere, and tables where people were gathered. Some were eating lunch, others were talking on their cell phones, and some were listening to music through small boom boxes. There were some children playing in the grassy area, and even a couple of dogs.

Over a three year period and more than a dozen visits to this medical office building I had never even realized this area existed. I had been so focused on my long drive, getting there on time, and parking close to the front entrance that I had completely missed the best part of this location. There was even a back exit onto a small street that would take me back to the freeway more easily, and I had never seen this, either.

I found it ironic that on this particular day my doctor released me, so I would never have a reason to return. Because I had worn blinders for all of that time, I had missed an opportunity to enjoy a beautiful setting that could have brought joy into my day on each visit.

Take the time to see things from a different perspective. Do this in every area of your life and the things you see will appear much differently to you.

Phase II - Laying The Foundation

"When it is obvious that the goal cannot be reached, don't adjust the goal, adjust the action steps." ~ Confucius

You will find Phase II to be the busiest one of the entire Weekend Marketer™ program. This is due to the fact that there is so much to set up to lay the proper foundation for your business. There will be times when you think it is just too much for you to do, but I promise that if you'll persevere and push through to accomplish everything I present here it will all pay off quite handsomely in a short time.

Also, when you work harder than you ever have before and learn many new things in a short period of time, you will be amazed later on at how you have changed. What I mean is that the next time you are presented with tasks and activities of this magnitude you will fly through them with the greatest of ease and wonder why you ever thought this was difficult or a challenge in the past.

This is also the phase where time management becomes a crucial piece of the puzzle. I like to share the story of 'Rocks, Pebbles, Sand' when I discuss this topic. Here it is:

A philosophy professor stood before his class with some items on the table in front of him. When the class began, wordlessly

he picked up a very large and empty plastic jar and proceeded to fill it with rocks, about 2 inches in diameter.

He then asked the students if the jar was full. They agreed that it was.

So the professor then picked up a box of pebbles and poured them into the jar. He shook the jar lightly. The pebbles, of course, rolled into the open areas between the rocks.

He then asked the students again if the jar was full. They agreed it was.

The professor picked up a box of sand and poured it into the jar. Of course, the sand filled up everything else.

He then asked once more if the jar was full. The students responded with a unanimous "Yes."

"Now," said the professor, "I want you to recognize that this jar represents your life. The rocks are the important things – your family, your faith, your health, your children – things that if everything else was lost and only they remained, your life would still be full.

The pebbles are the other things that matter – like your work, your house, your car.

The sand is everything else. It represents the small stuff."

"If you put the sand into the jar first," he continued "there is no room for the pebbles or the rocks. The same goes for your life.

If you spend all your time and energy on the small stuff, you will never have room for the things that are important to you. Pay attention to the things that are critical to your happiness. Play with your children. Take your partner out dancing. There will always be time to go to work, clean the house, give a dinner party and fix the garbage disposal.

Take care of the rocks first – the things that really matter. Set your priorities. The rest is just sand."

This model works well when you are changing your life in a major way. Use a calendar to plan out your next month. Have different colored markers to represent your rocks, pebbles, and sand. First, fill in your rocks – everything that you want and need to do that is related to your family, your faith, and your health. Just as we always pay ourselves first when we are entrepreneurs, we plan for the time we will spend with our 'rocks' before we plan anything else.

Next, use a different marker to schedule your work time and activities. This would include the hours you already work at your job, if that applies to you right now, as well as the hours you will be dedicating to your online business. I recommend that you allow ten to fifteen hours a week for laying your foundation to achieve best results. Your Quarterly Getaway (review Phase I) needs to be scheduled or you will soon find yourself feeling that you do not have the time to leave for an overnight stay.

Finally, write down everything else you like to do, such as going to the movies, watching television, or walking around your local shopping mall. This is all sand and can be adjusted and eliminated, at least in part, to make room for what is more important at this point in time in your life. During the first eighteen months I was online I did not go to the movies or out to eat more than a few times. I also turned off my television except for the occasional show I would record and watch later. Even though I missed these activities initially, once I started focusing on building my business I found that my life was more satisfying because I was engaged in something bigger, something that would change my future.

Delegate as much as possible. It's always difficult to let go of the control we have over some activities, such as grocery shopping, taking care of our car, mowing the lawn, cleaning the house, and even preparing meals. Once you let someone else 'own' these activities you will see just how much time it frees up for you to start your business. Yes, you will need to routinely check to make sure everything you have delegated is being handled in a way that is acceptable to you and that meets your standards and criteria, but finding competent help is extremely freeing.

One of the first things I delegated was going to the post office each week. I truly disliked taking the time to drive there and back and waiting in line when I had so many other things I preferred to be spending my time doing. I found the perfect person to do this for me, and she even drops off and picks up dry cleaning, goes to the store, and brings in my personal mail when she gets back to my house. This frees up about three hours each week, and she only charges me twenty-five dollars for the time it takes. It turns out she does this for two other people as well, so we all benefit from her service.

The Power Of Positive Self-Talk

Years ago my mother gave me a book called *What To Say When You Talk To Yourself* by Shad Helmstetter. It seemed pretty funny at the time, but when I finally read the book I realized that this was quite serious in nature and so important in my life. Over the years I have given this much thought, and now positive self-talk is a part of my morning routine that carries me through the day.

The idea is that we are all guilty of negative self-talk and must put an end to this so that we can enjoy optimal performance in every area of our lives. It's even been proven that our health and well-being is influenced by the messages we send to ourselves each and every day.

My personal experience with this concept was that I found myself becoming more and more negative each morning when I woke up. This was in late 2006 and into 2007, when I was working from home for the first time on a full time basis. Between six and six-thirty in the morning, when I had just woke up and let my dogs out, I would really beat up on myself by thinking about everything I had to do that day, what I had not completed the day before, and why everyone else was more capable and talented when it came to building an online business. One morning I caught a glimpse of myself in the bathroom mirror as I was having these thoughts and the person staring back at me was not someone I wanted to be.

Instead of feeling grateful and appreciative of the fact that I was now working from home, I was unhappy and unsatisfied with my life. I quickly took this book off the shelf in my office and began to consciously focus on positive self-talk and affirmations that I was doing the right things, taking the right actions, and changing my life in a way that would continue to bring me joy. Within a couple of weeks I was back on track and have been sharing this with my friends and business associates for years now.

Notice what you are saying when you talk to yourself throughout each day. Are you giving yourself positive reinforcement and patting yourself on the back for a job well done? Take a minute right now to look at yourself in the mirror and say something positive and helpful. If you find this to be a difficult task, start with something simple, like:

"You are wearing a nice shirt today. The color and fabric is perfect for this time of year and wearing it all day will make me feel comfortable and relaxed."

This may sound silly, or like something you don't need to do, but please know that your self-talk can help you to change your life and move forward by leaps and bounds if it is done on a daily basis.

If you have small children, or grandchildren, you know just how important it is to praise them for good behavior and choices every time you are with them. Well, it works in the same way for adults, and it all starts with the way to talk to yourself each day.

Do this every day and it will become a habit. This is part of the process of developing an entrepreneurial mindset for success!

Choosing A Niche

You can't get started if you do not know where you are going. Choosing a niche is crucial, and it must be the right one for you. However, you will change during your first year online and your niche will shift as well. This is how to choose a niche that will work for you during your first year:

Draw three large intersecting circles on a piece of paper. This is called a 'Three Circle Venn Diagram' and you may remember seeing it in math class while you were in school.

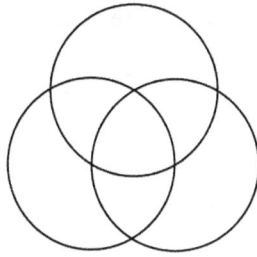

The circle on the left represents everything you enjoy, like to do, feel passionate about, and would be involved in regardless of whether there was money to be made. My circle includes spending time with my dogs, travel, photography, writing, and helping/teaching other people.

The circle on the right represents everything you have knowledge about. This would be training and education you have received, courses you have taken, certificates you have earned, and anything else you have learned on your own or through a job or career you've had. This circle would also include things you have learned as a result of your personal circumstances, such as caring for an elderly family member, dealing with cancer, or going through a job layoff.

The top circle represents the marketplace. This is where you must do some research to see what's available for sale in these areas. If most everything is already available free or at a very low cost, move on to another area. If many products, both digital and physical are available then you are on to a good one.

Where all three of these circles intersect is what I refer to as the 'sweet spot'. That is the niche market where you already have some knowledge, you enjoy spending time, and where there is a market to sell goods and service. You will be happiest if you work in the 'sweet spot' for at least a year.

The 3 Things You Must Have To Get Started

Getting started online is a way to work from home, or from wherever you happen to be. There is quite a bit of discussion as to how you can build a profitable and successful online business, but I believe in keeping it very simple. It turns out there are really only three things you need in order to start your online business. These are a domain name, hosting, and an autoresponder service.

A domain name provides you with the opportunity to set up a website that is owned and operated by you. I've seen too many people try to get started with their Internet business by using a site that belongs to someone else. While this offer of free space on the Internet may be tempting, steer clear and spend the ten dollars or so to register at least one domain name that is yours. Choose one that contains the keyword phrase that describes your niche, as well as one for your name to begin building credibility and visibility for yourself.

Your domain name must live somewhere, and that's where hosting comes in. there are several companies that offer what we need in order to do business online. This is referred to as c-panel, which is just short for control panel. This means that you can set up Wordpress on your domain with just a couple of mouse clicks, and that you will have access to everything you need when it comes to the technical side of the business. This typically costs about seven dollars each month for an unlimited number of domains, or seventy-five dollars a year if you choose to pay on an annual basis.

Finally, you will need an autoresponder service to build a list of interested prospects and to stay in touch with them through email. There are a few companies that offer this service, so choose one based on the recommendation of the coach or mentor you are working with. Spend some time going through the tutorials so that you will learn how to set up your emails and the mechanics of this process. Everyone makes mistakes in the beginning, so do not feel bad if this seems to be a confusing process.

Once you have your domain, your hosting account, and your autoresponder service you are ready to move into the next phase of running your business. This is the beginning of building a lucrative online business that will grow for years to come.

I wrote a Special Report with detailed information on what I have just shared here. You may download it at:

http://ConnieRagenGreen.com/reports/3things.pdf

Income generating activities are those that propel your business forward in a way that makes sense. Most of these marketing strategies will continue to work long after you have created and set them up the first time. Activities that you will want to be engaged in will include my 12 Steps for Getting Started Online:

1. *Choosing a niche*
2. *Blogging with your Wordpress site*
3. *Article marketing*
4. *Using PLR (Private Label Rights) Content*
5. *Public Domain*
6. *Writing Short Reports*

7. *List Building*
8. *Optin pages*
9. *Autoresponders*
10. *Traffic*
11. *Info product creation*
12. *Teleseminars*

I'll give you an introduction to each of these steps here, as well as how I have modified each one to suit you as a Weekend Marketer. Not having as much time as someone doing this full time means that you must proceed in a straightforward and deliberate way in order to stay focused and make progress quickly.

Choosing a niche – Your niche is the area you will work in and the people you will serve each day. For example, my niche is people who intend to leave their current job or those no longer in the work force who wish a build a profitable business on the Internet from their home computers. This sets me apart from people who work with people who want to use paid advertising to promote local businesses or people who design and build websites.

Choose a niche that you know something about and have an interest in or you will soon grow weary of the work involved to become successful. Look back at my earlier discussion on this here in Phase II where I showed you the picture of the three circle Venn diagram to work on this further.

Blogging - Your blog is your 'Home on the Internet'. I've been teaching this concept since 2006, yet few people make a commitment to using this powerful marketing tool and strategy to help them build a business more quickly.

If you feel that your don't have the time to blog, or that you will run out of things to talk about in your posts, read on for some ideas that will make a huge difference.

Ideas For Blog Posts:

- Current events – read newspapers, magazines, online articles, and anything else that will provide you with a ready source of material you can write about.

Blogging regularly, once and, hopefully, twice a week, will extend your visibility and increase your credibility in your niche. This content can then be leveraged in many ways, giving you a distinct advantage over your competition. It also will bring you many more leads and opportunities over time. Make a schedule for yourself, and include one ninety minute block each week that will be devoted exclusively to posting to your blog. I recommend you do this on Saturday morning, or forty-five minutes on Saturday and the other half of the time on one weekday evening each week. You'll decide when you have more creative energy for writing and schedule your blogging accordingly.

As a classroom teacher I knew that readers are writers, and that applies to online entrepreneurs as well. Spend time each week reading the other blogs in your niche, leaving comments, and getting some ideas for future posts. Tracking back to some of these posts will also bring you to attention from more established bloggers and others in your field, and you never know where that might lead.

I keep a small notepad next to my desk, and that's where I make notes on what I will be writing about in the future. That way, I only have to look at what I have written to get started right away with a new post. Sometimes I use the categories from my blog to decide what to write about. I simply go down the list and choose a new subject to fit each category.

You can get ideas for new blog posts from everyone you speak to, news articles, and even from social media. Over time you will even want to trade posts with others using something called guest blogging. This is an excellent way to increase your visibility and make lifelong connections with others in your niche.

During 2012 I began hosting a podcast each week. These thirty minute interviews, which are just casual conversations between me and others I have connected with, make for a great blog post each week. This is a way for me to add content to my site, while also tapping into the power of the iTunes channel to reach more people over time. People are much more likely to agree to be on my podcast because they see how much it has helped others.

Another strategy I've used twice now is to create an e-course as a blog post. I called it the 21 Day Productivity Challenge (you can read the entire e-course at: **http://21DayProductivityChallenge.com**), and added one item each day over a course of twenty-one days. Now I send people to that post so they can get started right away.

Article Marketing – I started writing short articles during 2006, and soon realized that this was an excellent way to create content in my niche, drive targeted traffic to my sites, build my list, and sell affiliate products and services.

In the spring of 2007 I challenged myself to write one hundred articles in one hundred days (I still own that domain - **http://100ArticlesIn100Days.com** and it goes to my course on this topic) and within a month I had turned myself into a writer. It only took me seventy-eight days to write those hundred articles, and my life changed forever as my business began to really take off in a way I had not expected.

Your articles must now have a minimum of four hundred words to be in line with the terms of service for most of the article directories, and I recommend keeping them between four hundred and five hundred words for best results. Anything longer and your reader may become bored and click away before reading your entire article and getting to the resource box at the end. This is where you are able to include a link to your own site where they may click over to become a part of your world by opting in to your list and downloading the free giveaway you have created for them.

PLR (Private Label Rights) – When I discovered that I did not have to personally create all of the content for my online business I literally jumped for joy. It turns out that you are able to purchase high quality writing on a wide variety of topics that can be used to help you build your online business. This is an excellent time saver, especially for weekend marketers. The only times you may never use PLR is when you are writing articles to submit to the article directories and when you are writing to publish a book, even on the Kindle or Nook. This is against the TOS (Terms of Service) in both cases.

I typically use private label rights content to create additional blog posts, especially for my niche sites, and for putting together short reports to give away and distribute widely.

Social Media – As I've shared with you, I started online in 2005 and 2006, and this was still the Dark Ages for social media. At that time Facebook was only for college students using an email address assigned to them by their school, Twitter did not go mainstream until 2007, and LinkedIn was a place for corporate types to connect with one another.

Once social media took off, everything changed in the world of online marketing. I believe these changes were positive, at least in most cases. People who were working alone from home suddenly had others to interact with, without having to leave the comfort of their home. When I had a question about something I was working on, there was always someone online who could give me a quick reply or a link to a resource that could help me further. On the other hand, many people became much less productive as they were consumed with spending time interacting with others instead of accomplishing the tasks they had set out to finish to build their businesses.

Short Reports – Once you are blogging and writing articles each week, you have the beginnings of a short report marketing funnel for your niche topic. I estimate that I have something like two hundred of these reports circulating on the Internet right now. Some of them are just four or five pages in length, while others are twenty-five or thirty pages long.

The idea with this marketing strategy is to break down your topic into smaller sub-niches where you can go into greater detail about what people want and need to know. There is a way to do this that will grow your list and earn you money from your own products you will create over time, as well as affiliate products you can recommend from within the report itself.

Start with a simple idea to see how it all works. For example, if your niche is helping people to be more productive and manage their time more efficiently, you may want to write one blog post and one article on this topic to share your best ideas.

List Building – You will begin to hear over and over that the 'gold is in the list'. It's actually in the list and the follow up you will do with your list, but it all begins with asking people to join your permission based list by giving you their name and email address in return for a free report or other giveaway you have prepared for them.

Remember that everyone starts out with no list at all, and that you can still earn lots of money with a very small list. My first book – *Huge Profits With A Tiny List: 50 Ways To Use Relationship Marketing To Increase Your Bottom Line* – became a bestseller simply because so many people were excited at the prospect of earning 6 figures a year or more with a list of just a few hundred names.

Target the exact people you want on your list, offer them a free giveaway they will be excited to receive, and your list will begin to grow.

Opt in pages – During my first two years working on the Internet I had people opt in to my list through a small signup box in the sidebar of my blog. It wasn't until I started working with a mentor that I realized just how much I was missing out on by not using opt in pages.

An opt in page is simple a single web page where a visitor has only two choices; they can either give permission to be added to your list by typing in their name and email address in return for your free giveaway, or they can click to exit the page altogether.

Opt in pages are extremely powerful as a way to build your list. They can be set up quite easily using Wordpress, or you can have someone create one for you using any program available for this purpose. Once you see how well these work your business will take off in a big way.

Autoresponders – The emails that are sent out automatically after someone joins your list are referred to as autoresponders. In the beginning, set up ten messages that will go out one per day for the first ten days someone is on your list. During this time you'll want to share your articles and blog posts, relevant tips and content, and make some offers of your own and affiliate products as well. People are the most excited and receptive during these days immediately after the sign up on your list, so you'll want to make the most of that by being in frequent contact with them.

Traffic – This term refers to the visitors that come to your pages and content on the Internet each day. There are three main techniques for driving traffic: *build* it, *buy* it, or *borrow* it. In the beginning you will build it by writing articles and blog posts, using SEO (search engine optimization) in everything you set up and write, and using free sites such as Squidoo.com to make your sites more attractive through back links (links that come back to your site from another location).

As you become a little more established you will be able to connect with JV (joint venture) partners and others who will help you to get the word out about your blog and other sites. Eventually you will be ready to buy traffic through a variety of advertising programs available, once you understand more of what is required to do this successfully.

Information Product Creation – It took me a full year of working online to create my first product. I simply had no idea what my market might want to buy from me, and felt inadequate when it came to creating a product and charging for it. My recommendation here is to jump in as soon as possible and create a one hour audio or video (as a webinar) where you teach and explain what you know. Create a short document to include as a PDF download, write a short sales letter, and put this out to the world as your first product. You can only improve what you can measure, and this product will be your starting point. Even if you make very few sales, this will give you the confidence to move forward. It definitely gets easier over time, but you will not have the experience unless you begin.

Teleseminars – In December of 2006 I enrolled in Alex Mandossian's Teleseminar Secrets course. This was a huge time and money investment for me at the time, and I was determined to improve my business with the training her was providing. By January of 2007 I had hosted my first teleseminar, and over an eighteen month period I went on to host one call each week. This proved to be the best way for me to gain confidence teaching in front of an audience, to present and refine my information, and to sell my own and affiliate products and services. This also made me more accessible to the people on my list and increased the all important 'know, like, and trust' factor.

Most of us host webinars these days, but I continue to use teleseminars twice a month to generate leads, sell more products, and to interact with my prospects and clients.

The 5 Pronged Approach™

My 5 Pronged Approach™ is a more simplified version of the 12 Steps to Getting Started Online that I have just presented to you. As a new online entrepreneur, think of this as a way to jumpstart what you are building before going back to do more. This will put you into the right frame of mind to see that you can indeed be successful with your business.

This approach includes blogging, article marketing, affiliate marketing, and social media.

Blogging – Your blog is your 'Home on the Internet, and as such, make sure it is inviting to your visitors. This means that you want to have your picture on the header or at least somewhere highly visible on the front page of your blog so that people can see what you look like. Be sure to add an 'About Me' page to share your mission and vision with your readers. Then, post regularly, at least once a week, to keep your site filled with fresh, relevant content that is your very best writing. The search engines will love you for doing this and over time you will have built up an authority site on your niche topic.

Article Writing and Marketing – I continue to find this the very best way to start creating content in your area that will serve you for years to come. Make a habit of writing something every day, even if you only have time for a couple of paragraphs, and then repurpose your writing into many different formats. After Google made the huge changes recently in regards to how they view content on the article directories, I now recommend that you not include your articles on your blogs as posts. Instead, keep your articles short and to the point and think of them as lead generators to build your list and idea starters for posts and other writing you will use forever.

Affiliate Marketing – I describe affiliate marketing as 'recommending what you love' and find that it's the very best way to start earning money in your new business. I only recommend and promote the products and services I have purchased, used, and benefitted from and suggest you do the same for best results. Start by writing a review of the product you want to promote as a blog post, and then rewrite that to use as an article to submit to the directories.

Teleseminars – I was so nervous about starting to host my own teleseminars my heart used to beat right out of my chest. Once I got used to speaking to my prospects each week on a call the nerves disappeared and I became a teacher.

Social Media – There was no social media when I got started on the Internet in 2005 and 2006, so once it took off I saw the immense benefit of including it in this approach. Connect with others, but only spend twenty minutes a day. That's more than enough time to share your knowledge and expertise with others and then you can get back to work.

During Phase II it is also the best time to start putting a 'dream team' together for your business. By this I mean that even though you will want to learn as much as possible about every aspect of what will be required, there is no possible way for you to become an expert in every part of it. Instead, look for people who play with the things you have to work at, such as creating graphics, website setup and design, technology in general, and bookkeeping. I started doing this within my first year and continue to work with some of these same people today.

Bartering is one way to pay for these services, so be sure to develop your expertise and skill in an area that will be valuable to others. As soon as I was able to write blog posts and articles with ease, I used this skill and talent to trade for the things I was struggling with.

Content Creation

Content creation was something I knew absolutely nothing about when I first came online. Almost overnight I found myself struggling to write articles, blog posts, and short reports. Once you get into the habit of creating content will give you an unlimited number of products to sell online. Creating your information product can be simple and quick when you follow these steps.

Do Your Research:

Before you even write a sentence of your information product, you should get your research done. I find the research component of my business to be quite enjoyable in that I am always learning something new. I also find resources that I will return to as I write more about my topic over the coming months and years. Get your research done before trying to write and you'll end up with a better product.

Organize With An Outline:

Getting organized is one of the most important parts of writing quickly. Your outline becomes a road map, and with it you are finally just filling in the blanks as you write about your topic. By writing out an outline first in order to organize your research, you will be able to work through your projects quickly. You won't have to stop and think about what to write next because you'll have your outline to follow and it will flow smoothly.

This is how I have been able to write so many books. Each one is based on an outline and I simply fill in the blanks until I am finished explaining and teaching my topic.

Use Storytelling To Share Your Experiences:

When I was first online I started sharing stories of what it had been like to work as a classroom teacher while also doing real estate part-time for the previous twenty years. This was the beginning of a content creation and marketing strategy known as storytelling, and I was not even aware of it at that time. I continue to use myself as a case study for everything I am able to achieve in my online business so that my students can learn from both my failures and my successes.

You will also want to share your lifestyle with your readers, so include some detailed information about what you do when you're not on the computer. I share the work I do with charities, my travels around the world, and my pets.

Don't Edit As You Write:

Our brains are complex organs, containing both creative and critical components. The critical side of your brain can get in the way when you are trying to write by getting you to stop and make changes after every thought you write down. Your writing will go faster and smoother if you can put your inner critic on the shelf and just write for a specific amount of time. You'll find that your writing will go more quickly when your critic is quiet during the writing process.

Once you have finished your writing for that period of time, then go back and read it out loud to decide what you need to change, edit, or rewrite.

Creating content online is the fastest way to building a profitable business if you are just getting started on the Internet. I have been quite prolific since coming online in 2006, but the truth is that I have worked a plan all this time that I will share here with you. Once I realized that my income was in direct proportion to how much content I could create I knew that I had to make this my focus each and every day.

The main issue for me was that I was not a writer at that time. It took dedication and hard work to turn myself into a writer, and you can do the same thing by following my example.

Your content, in the form of blog posts, articles, videos, audio recordings, short reports, eBooks, books for Kindle and Nook, and paperback books can be shared with your target audience around the world. This will help you to build the kind of relationships that take your business to the next level very quickly.

Here are some ideas to help you produce high quality content quickly and achieve far better results in your business consistently.

Carry a notebook with you every place you go. I always have one next to my bed, by my computer, in my purse, along the side of the seat in my car, and even in my kitchen! By making notes every day I always have a starting point for my writing. I generate ideas when I talk to friends and family members, read through magazines, read through my emails, and watch television. I write down two or three sentences so I know exactly what I was thinking at the time when I look back at my notebook days later. When I sit down to write, I already have a collection of ideas ready to go in my content creation endeavors.

Resist the urge to edit as you write or that will slow you down very quickly; instead, just let the writing flow. Whether I am writing in one of my notebooks or typing with two fingers (yes, that's correct) on the keyboard, I just keep moving and go back to reread and edit later on. When I was a classroom teacher I taught my students that writing is rewriting. That was a mistake. Instead, I should have taught them that writing is getting into the flow and allowing your thoughts to take shape on the paper or the screen. Ideas are everywhere, so be ready to tell stories about what you have encountered. My work with various charities and my pets are a ready source of stories for my business.

Readers are writers. Even though you may feel as though you do not have time to read while you are getting your business off the ground, take the time to read on a variety of topics. This will enhance your life and expand your knowledge base in a way that will manifest in your writing. I always have a paperback with me, as well as books on my iPad and Kindle.

I recently met a young man seated next to me on one of my flights. He had been an avid reader throughout school, and when he went to college he began to write. He told me that he had remembered what his parents had told him about 'readers are writers' and that's what gave him the confidence to pursue writing as a career. He was on his way to Los Angeles to take a job as an editor for a science fiction magazine while he wrote short stories, a screenplay, and articles for other magazines as a freelance writer.

Your prospects and clients will want to know as much about you as possible, so share stories that you are comfortable with sharing. I love to tell people about the charities I help, the places I travel to, and about what it was like when I was a classroom teacher and worked in real estate. I try to make a point with each story that makes it more interesting or even a learning experience. The key here is to always relate the stories and principles back to your original message.

You can also write a series of blog posts or articles on a particular topic. This was how I wrote my first book; I started writing a series of fifty ways to use relationship marketing to increase my bottom line. After a few months I had enough content for a one hundred and seventy page book!

Get your momentum going by writing nonstop for an hour to ninety minutes each day. My best time is first thing in the morning. I refer to this as my prime time for achieving the best results with my writing. Find your own 'prime time' and just start writing. Once you're flowing, don't stop. Keep going. As soon as the first article or blog post is done, start the next one. And keep it up until the inspiration is gone. Getting the momentum going is the hard part. You'll get much more accomplished if you just hold on when it's already moving for you.

My writing on any particular topic tends to end up being about four to five hundred words in length. This is the typical article or blog post so this fits my requirements very nicely. When I write something much longer, such as this post, for example, I know right away that I am going to repurpose it into many different formats. Shorter writing is fine; there's nothing wrong with one hundred fifty words if you can get your message across in that time frame. People have a very short attention span today, so shorter may actually be better as long as it is complete.

When people ask me questions I most always write them down in my notebook. This give me the impetus to write a longer answer that can be included in the content I will create that day or the next. If one person has the question, others will also. You can then publish the question (or at least the relevant portion) and the answer in your article.

I repurpose everything. Repurposing is the concept of turning your ideas into different formats to serve all types of learners – the visual, auditory, and kinesthetic ones. Publish your content on the social media sites, in short reports, on YouTube, in podcasts, and anywhere else you can think of for best results with this marketing strategy.

Repurpose Everything!

When I started writing articles in 2006 it was an arduous process. I spent about two hours on each one, making sure that I was presenting my topic in a way that could be easily understood by my readers. Articles were only required to be two hundred fifty words at that time, but it was still a struggle. I was using the ten tips style with each one, making a list of tips on my topic and then writing a couple of sentences about each one.

Each day I would start with a new topic, so this process started all over again. The result was that my business grew very slowly as I worked to come up with new ideas. That all changed when I discovered how to repurpose my articles into a variety of different formats to create an ongoing stream of content.

Repurposing is simply the process of taking your original idea and using it over and over in different ways. For example, you can write three articles, submit them to an article directory, and then turn them immediately into a short report. Even though the content is roughly the same, a whole new group of people will be able to learn from you when they receive your report.

This report may go on to become a new free giveaway to use when people opt in to your blog or other site. You will want to change it up a bit here, perhaps adding some action steps at the end and a page of related and appropriate resources.

Now it's time to think about different formats. Audio is used widely these days as a way to reach people who may not want to read, or those who are looking for information to take with them. Start by recording two or three minute audios and distributing them on sites such as AudioBoo (AudioBoo.fm), and the move on to using Internet radio sites (Blog Talk Radio is a good choice here) and to hosting your own teleseminars. Your prospects and clients will be able to listen to you talking about your topic by downloading it to their mp3 player and taking you on the road with them. There's nothing more exciting than hearing from your prospects and clients that you are in their iPod as part of their favorite playlist!

Video is equally important. You do not have to be in the videos yourself, but I do recommend giving that a try as well. I started by taking one of my articles and turning it into a slide presentation. I then recorded that by using the free software that came with my computer and then uploaded it to YouTube.
Repurposing your content will save you countless hours and get your content into the hands of many people who would otherwise not have access to the information you are sharing.

At this point in your progress I'd like to go into more details about the idea of *visibility*, *credibility*, and *profitability* in your online business. Even though I have touched upon some of this already, and will go into greater detail on becoming profitable in the next Phase of this program, let's discuss this concept now.

Credibility relates to who you are and what you stand for, in your personal life as well as your business. This is a good time to sit down with your family and talk about your Mission and your Vision statements. Wikipedia describes these as:

The key components of 'strategic planning' include an understanding of the firm's vision, mission, values and strategies. The vision and mission are often captured in a Vision Statement and Mission Statement.

Vision: outlines what the organization wants to be, or how it wants the world in which it operates to be (an "idealized" view of the world). It is a long-term view and concentrates on the future. It can be emotive and is a source of inspiration. For example, a charity working with the poor might have a vision statement which reads "A World without Poverty."

Mission: Defines the fundamental purpose of an organization or an enterprise, succinctly describing why it exists and what it does to achieve its vision. For example, the charity above might have a mission statement as "providing jobs for the homeless and unemployed".

Many people mistake the vision statement for the mission statement, and sometimes one is simply used as a longer term version of the other. However they are meant to be quite different, with the vision being a descriptive picture of a desired future state, and the mission being a statement of a business rationale, applicable now as well as in the future. The mission is therefore the means of successfully achieving the vision.

For an entrepreneurs or organization's vision and mission to be effective, they must become assimilated into the organization's culture.

I think about my mission as being what I intend to do in my business on an everyday basis. Mine is that I want to help people who are unemployed, underemployed, or dissatisfied with their current work situation to become online entrepreneurs to create a profitable and rewarding business.

My vision relates more to what I want for my future. That is to help people reach their highest potential and share their message with the world.

Credibility is what you will develop in order to become an expert in your niche. You notice I said *an* expert, not *THE* expert. *Think of this as becoming the authority on your topic.* In other words, you simply want to become one of the people in the world who is able to speak and write intelligently on your topic. Credibility gives you the ability to answer questions and solve problems for people who need and want to delve further into the area you are focusing on in your business.

You build credibility by spending time with a variety of activities on a regular basis. These would include, but are not limited to:

- Blogging on your topic – I blog two or three times a week, every week, to share my knowledge with others at (**http://HugeProfitsTinyList.com**).
- Writing short articles to submit to the directories – To date, I have written more than seventeen hundred articles that can be found all over the Internet.
- Writing short reports – I continue to write a new short report each month on a different aspect of my business.

- Publishing your writing to Kindle and other sites – I have many books available (**http://ConnieLoves.me/AuthorPage**) and continue to write regularly.

- Hosting teleseminars and webinars – Twice a month I host a free teleseminar and I regularly host webinars to teach my topic to others. (**http://AskConnieAnything.com**)

- Sending press releases – Start with free press releases to get used to sharing your information in this way, and then switch over to the paid services for maximum results with this.

- Speaking locally and around the country/world – I began my speaking career by practicing at my local Rotary Club. Soon I was asked to present to the Rotary District meeting, which meant speaking in front of several hundred people. In 2008 I was asked to speak at a conference for online marketers in Atlanta, Georgia, and now I speak almost every month somewhere in the world.

Visibility is concerned with how easily people are able to find you when they are searching for what you do and what you have to offer. The idea here is to have people tell you they see you 'everywhere' when it comes to your niche and areas of expertise. I have been able to increase my visibility dramatically with:

- Social media – I start threads on Facebook to get people talking, interacting, and sharing, while viewing me as the thought leader.

- Attending live events – Since 2006 I have attended more than fifty live events. My recommendation is to choose two or three a year and see which ones feel right for what you want to achieve in your business.

- Being active on select forums – I am a member of three paid forums and spend about one hour total each week with reading and posting to these. The free forums are a waste of time these days, so choose one or two paid ones that make sense for your niche. Your signature line introduces you to the members so that you do not need to ever fell like you are self-serving while you are there. Simple ask and answer questions and provide resources to the other members to let them know that you are knowledgeable and truly care.

- Hosting my own podcast series on iTunes – I started a podcast series at the beginning of 2012 and have experienced tremendous visibility with this strategy. I've also connected with people I may have never met otherwise. Challenge yourself to get started with this and then follow through with your commitment. You will be amazed how quickly you are noticed when you add this strategy to your online business.

- Adding my books to Kindle and Nook – These sites are huge, and the people who find me here would most likely not have found me through any other channels. These days I write every single day, and by repurposing everything I do I end up with massive original content for these books I want to publish. Some of mine are also in paperback, but the digital versions always outsell the physical ones.

- Interviewing others and requesting interviews – I used to hesitate when someone wanted to interview me; now I see it as a gift and an opportunity to get my name out to the world. Choose two topics you can speak on and make yourself a short outline for each one. Over time you will learn which one is better received by your prospects and clients and you can develop it into a full presentation, a short online course, and a book.

- Syndicating my content – You can use RSS feeds and Facebook's Networked Blogs application to expand your reach for global distribution. This simple process will enable you to find so many more people who will be interested in you and what you are doing online. RSS stands for 'really simple syndication' and allows us to share our content more easily than ever before.

- Making videos to add to my YouTube Channel – When I finally decided I was ready for my close-up, this became lots of fun and great visibility for me and for my business. You can choose to be in your videos or do screenshots. I mix mine up to keep it interesting. You can visit my Channel at: **http://YouTube.com/ConnieRagenGreen**.

Profitability is the component that makes this a business. Without making the effort each day to earn money from what you are doing, you are nothing more than a volunteer. Now there is nothing wrong with that, but you must make the distinction up front before you can proceed any further.

My goal when I came online initially was to be able to replace the income I had been earning while I was a classroom teacher, real estate broker, and residential appraiser. I had a large house payment, a car payment, and other expenses, and this was intended to become a full time business for me. Little did I know at that time that I could earn so much more, but that was not my focus during the early days.

I decided to set a goal for myself of earning one hundred dollars each day. Even though this would not be enough to pay my bills, I felt that I had to start somewhere. I'll be going into more details on this in Phase III. For now, just think about the ways you will be able to earn money online, whether you are working at your computer, sound asleep, or on vacation far away from your home.

You have now laid a proper foundation for your business and will be able to build upon this forever. We will now move into next phase where we will embrace the idea of monetization more fully.

Phase III – Monetization

When you find something that is more important to you than anything material, or even tangible that helps you to reach your potential, you can become more confident and have less fear. Acknowledge what is human about you and then express it and project it in a creative and artistic way. ~ Lady Gaga

The fun, and peace of mind, really begins when you start to earn even a small amount of money with your online business. This was my first experience with being able to creatively decide how to earn money since my days as a teenage entrepreneur I shared with you near the beginning of this book.

You'll want to get started by figuring out exactly how much money you need to earn each day in order to pay your bills. For me that number was three hundred thirty dollars a day, thirty days a month, so that I could cover all of my expenses. That sounded next to impossible when I was just getting started, even though I can see now that it wasn't impossible at all, so I decided to use $100 a day as my beginning goal at that time. I then focused on finding ways to earn that much each day, even though I was only working actively ten or fifteen hours a week in the very beginning.

That's how I got started with affiliate marketing. I saw that by recommending other people's products and services there would be an endless inventory to sell. It also taught me that I should be very picky when it came to recommending something that was not my own. Recurring products were very appealing because you recommend them once and get paid over and over again.

Profit Funnels for Multiple Streams of Online Income

Are you creating 'multiple streams of online income' for yourself and your family? When I think about how I have set up and built my online business over the past few years I realize that I've created eight separate profit funnels that bring me multiple streams of income on a regular basis. This was not my intention in the beginning, but as I continued to learn and implement what was available to me as an online entrepreneur these were the eight areas I resonated with and added to my funnel one at a time. Each funnel brings me a profit stream that has helped me to be successful on the Internet with a lucrative business I can run from home, or from wherever I happen to be. These profit funnels include:

- Affiliate marketing
- Local business marketing
- My own products and courses
- Services I offer to others
- Membership sites
- Niche sites

- Amazon

- Coaching

Affiliate marketing was the very first way I was able to earn money online. Because I had no product of my own and was just starting to blog and write articles, it made sense for me to recommend the products and courses I was benefitting from to others who were also getting started online. I earned my first affiliate commission in April of 2006 and have never looked back.

Then, because I was learning how to market on the Internet and honing my skills, I began helping a friend to market his insurance business and a family member get started with a handyman business. This was my first attempt at local business marketing and since that time I have even created a course where others can learn how to do this as well. Small businesses everywhere need our help so they can stay in business and thrive in any economy.

Actually, I began helping small businesses to get the word out about their services quite by accident. During that first summer I was working online, one of my family members started a handyman business. He had been layed off by his company a few months earlier, and then had an old back injury start to act up on him again. He was almost sixty years old, so he and his wife decided that he could open up a handyman business out of his garage and do small repairs for people in their local area who needed this type of help around the house. He loved meeting new people, had a real knack for fixing things, and already owned many tools, so his handyman service was born.

The problem came when he needed to get more customers. His friends and neighbors had been very supportive of his new business, but they just didn't need his help with anything else that summer. He began advertising in his local newspaper at a cost of almost five hundred dollars a month. This brought in some business, but it would take up to two weeks before he was in the black after paying so much for the ad.

Towards the end of the summer I found out what he was doing and offered to help him market his services to the community. He was more than happy to buy the domain name I suggested, along with a hosting account. I set up a blog for him, made some posts, and added some pictures of him installing a ceiling fan and repairing a kitchen faucet.

Within a month he was getting calls and had cancelled the newspaper advertisement. People were finding his blog through Google and the other search engines and calling him to make appointments. He and his wife were so excited about this they began to tell others, including the man we both had our car insurance with. He offered to hire me to help him get more business and my local marketing service took off in a big way.

By the end of my first year online I had created my first product and added this to my profit funnel. This first product was a four part course on how to use blogging and article marketing to increase your visibility, credibility, and profitability. Even though only ten people signed up for the live course, I was very excited about being a teacher again. Each week I hosted a teleseminar (webinars were not so common in 2006) and shared my information with the students. I also prepared a short Study Guide for each session that included an outline of what I was going to teach, as well as some resources.

This course sold for ninety-seven dollars and taught me that having my own line of products would increase my affiliate income while also adding another stream of income to what I was putting in place. In fact, I decided to create another four module course just as soon as this first one was finished, and then gave it as an unannounced bonus to my current students. This turned out to be a win-win and I learned so much in the process.

Helping others get set up online led me to my next area of income production. Soon I was offering my services to others, such as installing plugins and setting up Wordpress blog. Even though this involved trading time for money, I saw it as an opportunity to start outsourcing some of the tasks to others. Having someone help me with small tasks made me much more comfortable asking with asking others to assist me on a regular basis with even larger tasks.

In 2008 I added membership sites to the mix. I learned that I could add information and training each month to a membership site and that many people would be willing to pay by the month to receive this information. I continue to use the membership site model in my business.

Niche sites soon followed, and I still enjoy the process of choosing a hobby or interest of mine and setting up a site that will earn income for years to come. There are so many possibilities for this. I even have family members who earn online income based on their interests in model trains, skateboarding, fashion accessories, and relationships.

In 2010 I wrote and published my first book, *Huge Profits With A Tiny List: 50 Ways To Use Relationship Marketing To Increase Your Bottom Line*. It quickly became a #1 bestseller and changed the way others perceived me. This book is available on

Amazon and Barnes & Nobel in both paperback and Kindle formats. This led to my writing several more books as I saw the profit potential and personal satisfaction of creating an income stream with Amazon. I think of Amazon as a distribution channel that brings in more leads and referrals from people who otherwise may have never found me.

I also run a coaching program. I refer to this as mentoring, rather than coaching, for a few reasons. A mentor takes a few people under their wing and helps to guide them towards success. I only work with twelve people each year and love the way I can be a part of the progress someone makes over time.

Which of these profit funnels are you already using? I recommend making a study of what is possible as an online entrepreneur and then jumping in to get started.

Recurring Income for Residual Online Income

The recurring income model is the best way to build up your residual online income stream. I learned this very quickly when I was just getting started online and continue to focus on this model six years later. I am talking about doing a promotion for a product or service where you will receive ongoing commissions for as long as someone remains an active member.

There are many products and services that require a monthly fee for recurring service. Some of these include membership sites, teleseminar services, shopping carts, and programs where we are billed monthly. Just take a look at your latest credit card statement to see which ones you are being billed for each month. Now imagine if you were able to recommend these same services to others in return for a healthy commission.

I will use the shopping cart service as an example. Everyone doing business on the Internet needs a shopping cart of some kind. This service can be paid for either monthly or annually and the companies that provide it are happy to pay commissions for the life of the new customer. Your goal is to bring new people in to a service you already know and use so that you can build up your commissions over time. You will recommend it to someone once and be paid for years to come, as long as that person remains a customer.

You can recommend this service in a variety of ways. I like to start with a short report that gives some information on the service and goes into more detail as to how it works and why someone would want to choose this service over another one that is similar. Many times the company even has material prepared that you will be able to use in your report. Always give credit to the person or group that prepared this information to respect the copyright laws. Be sure to include your affiliate link in the report and explain to your readers that this means you will be receiving a commission should they decide to purchase.

Now it's time to distribute this report widely. Give a downloadable copy to everyone you can possibly reach to teach them the value of using this particular shopping cart over another. Another method I use is to teach people how to use the product or service, in this case the shopping cart, by hosting regular calls where I can answer their questions. Record the calls and give them out to anyone new who signs up through your affiliate link. Your residual income stream will grow over time as you build your business using this model.

There are so many possibilities for monetizing the work you will do online. If you always come from the place of wanting to serve others with your time, knowledge, and expertise, you will find many creative and lucrative outlets for your ideas.

Phase IV - Expert Status

Go confidently in the direction of your dreams. Live the life you've imagined. ~Henry David Thoreau

If you are a generalist in your niche, you can only expect to have limited results. If you become a specialist your results will increase, but only to a certain degree and level. However, if you are willing to do what it takes to become an expert on your topic, the world will be at your doorstep to learn from you and do business with you for many years to come. Reading every day is a crucial part of this process. According to Brian Tracy, reading just one hour a day in your chosen niche will put you at the top of your field within just three years. You can speed up that process by reading and studying for at least two hours each day, and this is what I have continued to do since 2006. Considering that about eighty percent of all adults have not read a book from beginning to end during the past year.

Let's take a look at how you can work on achieving the coveted expert status in the shortest amount of time.

What I am describing in this phase of the Weekend Marketer program is the use of 'channels' to help you to be perceived as an expert on your niche topic by the people who are searching for more information on what you have to offer. These channels include

Amazon, iTunes, YouTube, and social media, and they are just a starting point for what you will be doing to get your name and message out to the world.

The very best way, in my opinion, to be viewed as an expert is to write a book on your topic and use yourself as a case study. I have done this several times now with excellent results. Start taking regular notes on what you are achieving, and then turn these notes into articles, blog posts, and short reports that can finally be put together as a book.

With the recent availability of so many outlets for self-publishing, you will have your choice for publishing and distribution, including Amazon's Create Space program for paperback books and Kindle and Nook for digital versions. I would not recommend that you sell your book as an eBook on a separate web page because this would detract from what you want to accomplish here, and is also not permitted if you involved in the Kindle Select Program. Stick with the more acceptable distribution channels for fast and effective results.

Next, begin speaking about your topic. Start with local venues, such as Rotary and Kiwanis clubs, Chamber's of Commerce, real estate boards, and trade association meetings. Prepare a short presentation and a handout to use at these meetings. Then move on to Internet radio by letting people know that you are available to be interviewed on your area of expertise. You may want to hire an assistant to help you get booked, or use social media to reach out to those who would be interested in hosting you.

Finally, begin hosting your own teleseminars and podcasts. I did this each week for eighteen months when I was getting started, and continue to do it once or twice a month to stay connected with my prospects and clients. Allowing people to hear your voice is the next best thing to being there in person to look them in the eye and shake their hand. Many people find me on iTunes through my podcast series.

An additional distribution channel to help you attain expert status is YouTube. I make short videos that share my lifestyle and connect me with my target audience. My recommendation here is to keep your videos under three minutes in length in most cases, and to use a variety of settings and techniques to share your message in this way.

You will find that the more you read, write, and talk about your topic, the greater knowledge and understanding you will have about it. It won't take long for you to be considered a foremost leader in your field.

Getting Started

Recently one of my students came to stay at my home for three days. During this time we did have lots of fun, but we also accomplished quite a bit when I shared my strategy with him on how to promote an affiliate product so that it will sell on a regular basis without you having to be there each day. This is the list I had ready for him when he arrived:

1. Write an article – 400-500 words – submit it to EzineArticles – Topic: a product you are currently promoting as an affiliate

2. Create a short report from one of the PLR packs that will allow you to discuss and incorporate the product listed in #1 above

3. Find an interesting post on my blog at **http://HugeProfitsTinyList.com** and leave a comment

4. Based on #3, write a 300-400 word post on your own blog and trackback back to my post

5. Add a KindleIt (**http://connieLoves.me/KindleIt**) button with a report on any one of your posts and share it with your list and on social media

6. Write and schedule an email to your list to go out by 8 am EST on Monday that promotes your blog and the affiliate product

7. Reach out to someone you would like to connect with and contact them in 3 ways:

    • On social media

    • Through an email or their support desk

    • Using snail mail with a handwritten card

    • Then, tell them what you have in mind

8. Choose an all new product to promote next week and build a campaign around it with:

    • An article

- A blog post

- A short report

- Social media

- An audio recording

- This will all be done next week, not this weekend

- Choose the product from Clickbank, JVZoo, or from someone you have not promoted before

9. Be CREATIVE with this and HAVE FUN!

10. I will be doing the exact same thing while you are here

This turned out to be both fun and profitable, and my student told me that he saw online marketing in a new light after spending this time with me.

Attending Live Marketing Events

I have been attending live marketing events for years, and have now been to lots of them. When I say 'lots' I mean that I have been an attendee or a speaker at more than sixty live marketing conferences and seminars since 2008. During this time I have learned so much, including how to behave and carry yourself when you are at a business conference.

You must remember, first and foremost, that you are there to build your business. Even though there will be many opportunities to socialize over the course of the event, your goals must remain to be the focus of what you are there for and wish to achieve. It's not your cousin's wedding or your neighbor's barbeque; these events are meant to help you further your knowledge and reach new heights in your overall business plan in a much shorter time frame than you could do on your own.

With that said, here are three things that I observe regularly when I am at conferences and seminars across the United States:

Imbibing Too Much - This is the number one way to ruin your reputation in a business setting. Even if you would normally have a drink when out with friends, keep it to a minimum while you're at a conference. I have business associates who like to drink wine in the evenings, so I always graciously accept one glass and then sip it slowly all evening. This makes me 'one of the group' without having to compromise my beliefs or defend actions later on. My friend Jim Lafferty, a Coca-Cola® CEO in Asia and Africa, recently recounted a story on this topic when we were both speaking at a conference in Toronto, Canada. He feels even more strongly than I do about the effect overdoing it can have on the rest of your career. He shared how someone in this situation ended their career because of poor judgement in a public setting.

Sloppy Personal Appearance – We all judge a book by its cover, even if we think we keep an open mind in this area. T-shirts with witty phrases and controversial pictures give people a negative opinion of you right away. I visit several cities regularly, such as

Austin, Texas and Atlanta, Georgia, and have shirts I purchase at the airport or the hotel gift shop with the name of the city on them. I typically wear these on the night I arrive to show my support for natives of that city. Also, clothing that gives you the 'dishevelled' look is simply not acceptable. If your clothing looks like you've slept in it, it isn't appropriate for what you are working to achieve as a credible business person.

Sharing Sensitive Personal Values And Beliefs – A business conference is definitely not the place to share personal stories in regards to race, religion, politics, sexual orientation, or previous employment, even if there is a point to your story. I have seen people embarrass themselves by sharing personal information with a group that would have been best left for a private conversation. If you even suspect that it might be 'TOO MUCH INFORMATION', keep it to yourself unless you are only sharing it with one other person who may need to have access to these intimate details.

When I brought these three points up to one of my students his response was to cite examples of what others were doing that did not follow the guidelines I'm setting forth here. It doesn't matter what anyone else is doing. You must take full responsibility for your choices and actions. You may recall when your mother said something to you like, "If everyone else jumped off the building, would you line up to be next?" She was right.

Instead, use these events as an opportunity to present yourself in a professional and positive way. Choose clothing that fits you well, is made of materials that breathe, and that stays looking good even after sitting for long periods of time. Drink in extreme moderation, or not at all. Only share stories that will build your reputation and show you off in a positive light later on when repeated to others. Yes, everything you drink, wear, or say is likely to be repeated to others, so make sure it will help you to achieve your goals instead of stopping you in your tracks. Make the most of attending live marketing events and it will be reflected in your credibility and your bottom line.

Section Three

Be willing to do what others will not for the next twelve months; be able to live the way others cannot, forever.

~Connie Ragen Green

Section Two of this book outlined the four phases of The Weekend Marketer™ course in great detail so that you will be able to get started right away. In this final section I will discuss how you can apply these very same principles to your life in general, no matter what you are doing to make a living and at which point along the continuum you happen to be at the current time.

In Phase I we took an up close and personal look at mindset, confidence, and time management strategies. Putting yourself into the right frame of mind each and every day is crucial to your success in life. No matter where you are right now, you can devote some time to yourself each day to uplift your thinking. I call this 'quiet time', and it is my time to think, reflect, and plan out my day. Thirty minutes is sufficient for this; do what works best for you. If you have immediate responsibilities when you arise, such as attending to pets, children, or others, take care of that first and then retreat into solitude for half an hour to gather your thoughts and move into your quiet space. This will help you to be more productive and happier for the remainder of your day.

Building up your confidence must also become a daily habit. Find what feeds and nourishes your soul and linger there each day. I find that an early morning walk is the perfect way to get me into the space of appreciation, forgiveness, and gratitude. This is when I think about my activities for the day and give myself a little 'pep talk' about my expectations for myself. This also gives me a chance to review whatever I will be doing to see if I am fully prepared for what it to come.

We also explored the concept of managing your time during Phase I. I believe the topic of time management is so important that I co-authored a book on it in September of 2012. Geoff Hoff and I wrote a full length manuscript (almost twenty thousand words), edited, formatted, and published it during a seven day period. The title of this book, which continues to be well-received by readers and critics, is *Time Management Strategies for Entrepreneurs – How to Manage Your Time to Increase Your Bottom Line.* It went to bestseller status within the span of one day, putting us at the #1 position in two separate categories. One of the reasons we decided to write this book, and to do it so quickly from start to finish, was to share our techniques for thinking and acting in a productive way that does not take up all of your precious time.

In Phase II laying the foundation for your online business was our focus. This is the Phase I consider to be the busiest one in terms of getting everything set up for your business. Do not become discouraged or overwhelmed if it takes you longer than you originally anticipated to move through this part of the process. Instead, allow yourself more time while staying focused on your goals and dreams.

In Phase III monetization was explored. In order for your business to succeed, it must be profitable. Allow yourself to be creative when it comes to the business model(s) you will choose and how you will go about implementing them each day. Become a creative thinker and do not limit yourself to what others are doing or to what you observe to be the status quo. Strive for excellence as you have fun with the monetization of what you are building.

In Phase IV gaining expert status was the main focus. Being able to stretch yourself into a mind-shift and evolution of the person you are becoming will be very exciting during this Phase. Imagine going to the very outer limits of what you ever thought was possible and moving into your new skin.

The Four Stages of Competence

What I am about to share with you took me quite by surprise when I first studied it during 2006. It's the widespread idea of needing to go through four stages to reach the point where we can achieve our life goals more easily.

In psychology, the four stages of competence, or the "conscious competence" learning model, relates to the psychological states involved in the process of progressing from incompetence to competence in a skill.

Initially described as "Four Stages for Learning Any New Skill", the theory was developed at the Gordon Training International by its employee Noel Burch in the 1970s. It has since been frequently attributed to Abraham Maslow, although the model does not appear in his major works.

The Four Stages of Learning provides a model for learning. It suggests that we as individuals are initially unaware of how little we know, or are unconscious of our incompetence. As we recognize our incompetence, we consciously acquire a skill, then consciously use that skill. Eventually, the skill can be done without consciously being thought through completely, and the individual (us) is said to have unconscious competence.

Several elements of this model, including helping someone 'know what they don't know' or recognize a blind spot in one or more aspects of their life, may be related to age and life experiences, while the four stages of competence deals with the different learning stages.

The first of these is:

Unconscious Incompetence

The individual does not understand or know how to do something and does not necessarily recognize the deficit. They may deny the usefulness of the skill. The individual must recognize their own incompetence, and the value of the new skill, before moving on to the next stage. The length of time an individual spends in this stage depends on the strength of the stimulus to learn. When it comes to being an entrepreneur, this is the stage where we have not yet realized that making these changes in our life will be beneficial for a variety of reasons.

Conscious Incompetence

Here is where we are aware of the fact that there are many things we simply do not know. This can be frustrating at any age or in any situation, but this struggle is necessary to the process of moving on to the next steps in our life.

Though the individual does not understand or know how to do something, he or she does recognize the deficit, as well as the value of a new skill in addressing the deficit. The making of mistakes can be integral to the learning process at this stage.

As an entrepreneur this is in direct correlation to how you proceed and take action with everything you are learning. By not implementing your new skills, you risk remaining stagnant and unable to move on.

Conscious Competence

The individual understands or knows how to do something. However, demonstrating the skill or knowledge requires focus and concentration. It may be broken down into steps, and there is heavy conscious involvement in executing the new skill.

In your new business, strive for daily action to reinforce what you are doing. It's a new world, and you must rise to the occasion by staying focused, asking many questions, connecting with the right mentor for you, and keeping a written journal of your achievements.

Unconscious Competence

The individual has had so much practice with a skill that it has become "second nature" and can be performed easily. As a result, the skill can be performed while executing another task. The individual may be able to teach it to others, depending upon how and when it was learned.

I first used this strategy while I was in the classroom, and continue to do it today; I teach a concept and then ask one of my students to teach it to someone else. The greatest success with this is achieved when you move quickly from mastering a skill to teaching it to someone else.

Find friends, neighbors, or family members to practice on. Many of them will be thrilled to learn from you, and the result will be a chain of teaching, exchanging ideas, and engagement you will benefit from for years to come.

Final Thoughts

I sincerely hope that this book has given you food for thought and, at the very least, the understanding that you can achieve anything you want to by simply making the conscious decision to change your life. You can grow by leaps and bounds if you are willing to accept the challenge and move forward, willingly and confidently, each and every day.

Making the decision to leave the job or career you have worked at for many years and come on the Internet to start working as an online entrepreneur is one that will change your life forever. When I dd this back in 2006 I had no idea of what was to come about over the next few years. I do believe that anyone can make this change in their life, but you must take the necessary steps to make sure you are building a business that will sustain you for years to come. This requires hard work as you create your content, build a list, increase your visibility, and set up the systems that will bring the profitability necessary for a successful business online.

My recommendation is that you go back over each section of this book and through each Phase of the Weekend Marketer™ program at least one more time before embarking on your personal journey. Make lots of notes, research sites I have mentioned, and join my list by going to **http://WeekendMarketer.com**.

I am reminded of the often quoted Chinese Proverb, "If you give a man a fish you feed him for a day. If you teach a man to fish you feed him for a lifetime." I believe this is perfectly aligned with what this book is all about; by my teaching you how to build an online business to become an entrepreneur and live the life you love, I have given you food for a lifetime.

About the Author

Connie Ragen Green works with new online entrepreneurs on six continents, helping them to build a profitable online business from their home computer. A former classroom teacher and real estate broker/appraiser, Connie now works exclusively online. This enables her to travel the world, to speak at a variety of seminars and conferences, and to stay involved with and volunteer for several non-profit organizations and charitable foundations.

To find out more, please visit her main site at:
http://HugeProfitsTinyList.com

To learn more about making the transition from where you are today to becoming an online entrepreneur, be sure to visit:

WeekendMarketer.com

This site has been designed with you in mind, and will give you access to more information and resources as you begin your journey. It is my goal and intention to help you with this process in any way I possibly can.

Connie Ragen Green